# UNDETERRED

How One Determined Vietnamese Orphan
Carved Out a Place for Himself in America

## BRUCE CARLIN

UNDETERRED
by Bruce Carlin

Published by 3Niñas Publishing

Cover design by Jana Rade

Library of Congress Control Number: 2022907294

ISBN:     979-8-9856227-1-3 Paperback edition
          979-8-9856227-2-0 Hardcover edition
          979-8-9856227-0-6 Digital edition

Printed in the United States of America

v19

# DEDICATION

*Undeterred* is dedicated to people who arrived from somewhere else.

It is dedicated to those who braved a journey from another country to better their lives, looking for a more prosperous tomorrow for themselves and their families.

Immigrants make this country great. The diversity of backgrounds, values, and talents blend together to make the United States a robust society. We're not of one place of origin. We're not of one belief. We're not of one religion. We're not of one set of genes.

We are a melting pot of beautiful differences and yet, we are the same.

Long is one of those immigrants, and this book is dedicated to him and all like him who have built this country into what it is today.

# CONTENTS

# CHAPTER 1

---

# ATTACK

*I have to jump off this bridge. The smoke's black. My chest hurts. They're coming. Will the water hurt...can I jump like big kids...will I break my legs, die? Too far down to the water. But the tanks, they're coming. The ground is shaking. The rockets too close—the whistling and screaming is making me deaf. I'm afraid.*

Duc, in the water below, yelled: "Jump, little brother, jump! You saw me, I'm fine, see? Do like I did."

Balanced on the cracked concrete wall at least twenty feet above, Long fought against the heavy, black wind, bird-thin legs shaking; from the corner of his eye, he could see the tanks approaching but could not move, the green-brown water so far below, so far down.

"I can't, Duc! I can't!" He hopped from his perch, scurried to the end of the bridge. The noise seemed to chase him as he slid down the steep hill—bushes scratching his bare chest as he dropped into the water with the other kids. "Do you see the tanks and rockets?" squealed Long.

"They're coming here! We can't stay. They'll get us. I don't want to die."

The approaching tanks announced their arrival with a loud grinding noise as they ripped up the streets. Rockets landed perilously closer as the jets overhead moved into dive formation. Duc crouched as he neared the bank, turning to locate Long whose head and shoulders were just above the vibrating surface of the water, the ripples telegraphing the rumble of the tanks. He knew – they had to run.

The New York Times

*April 28, 1975*
### Saigon Hears the Fighting at Its Edge
*By FOX BUTTERFIELD*

SAIGON, South Vietnam, Monday, April 28 — A heavy column of black smoke rose over the edge of Saigon today as advance Communist forces moved close to the city limits.

South Vietnamese Air Force helicopters fired rockets into the Communist positions on the Saigon River at Newport, a former United States port complex on the road to Bien Hoa. The Communists fired back with AK-47 automatic rifles, and the noise audible inside the city.

Only a few lightly armed South Vietnamese combat policemen and militiamen guarded the road on the northeastern edge of the city. They made no effort to dig in, and several Government officers simply stood around watching the helicopters firing at the Communist forces.

## Seize End of Bridge

The Communist troops, who seized the far side of the Newport Bridge over the Saigon River, believed to be part of major North Vietnamese units moving rapidly toward Saigon from Bien Hoa, 15 miles to the northeast. Another group of Communist troops occupied a crossroads two miles beyond the bridge on the way to the biggest South Vietnamese ammunition dump, at Cat Lai.

The Communist advance blocked all traffic at the large Hang Xanh intersection, the main gateway to Saigon from the north. Combat policemen wearing flak jackets, helmets and mottled green and brown uniforms stood behind barbed-wire barricades, forcing all traffic back into the city.

It was the closest fighting to Saigon since the Communists' Tet and spring offensives of 1968.

## CHAPTER 2

---

# BEFORE

Soldiers had always been part of his life. When soldiers came to the village, Long's stomach felt empty even though he had eaten, his heart and head pounded. He watched them, lying low to blend in. "Duc, the soldiers are coming. We need to hide."

Duc grabbed Long, ran beyond the huts into the greenery, slipping below the giant, wet, green leaves, which covered them and tickled their backs. A few bugs found refuge on their bodies as they tried to stay still. The wet earth of their hiding spot had a welcome smell, the smell of cover.

*Why are they fighting?* thought Long. "Why do they take the boys?" questioned Long urgently. Duc didn't answer, just kept low and watched. Few men lived in the village, other than the elders. Soldiers gathered up the older kids, handed each a rifle—child-boys, now soldiers.

None went willingly.

They knew what it meant—they would not survive.

When soldiers approached, the women tried to hide their sons in tunnels. Mothers acted fast and instinctively but could not hold back their tears, fearing that they'd never see their boys again. They knew that their sons would be on the front line, put there with no preparation and no chance—just a body to hold a rifle.

The South's army was a patched together force. The North Vietnamese and Viet Cong armies, meticulously trained in stealth operations, weapons, and hand-to-hand combat, were well-prepared to face off with 12-year-olds pulled from their mothers' arms. If the women couldn't get the boys to the tunnels in time, they bartered with cigarettes, and sometimes more. Camel cigarettes were the most valuable—the packaging pictured a camel that no one had ever seen. When cigarettes were not enough, the mothers offered themselves in return for their boys' freedom.

*Enjoy the bridge, play, see how big a splash I can make, because when I'm old enough, I'm going to be taken away,* Long reasoned. He had a sense of urgency to grow up and jump into the water, but not to grow up too fast because *I'll end up with a rifle in my hands.*

Long wore a found pair of shorts and no shirt—sandals, when he could find some. His first came from his big brother Duc, found on a dead kid, smelly and sticky with blood on them. Long watched as Duc pulled off the shoes from the mutilated body. Long looked at the boy's face, half of it gone, bullet holes marking his body—the boy, not much older than Duc.

"I hope that this boy did not suffer. I am sorry about him being killed, but I am happy to have his sandals."

Duc looked at him and wondered how Long could feel so much compassion for this kid, a stranger. *After all, he's got stuff we need*, Duc thought. Frustrated with the stickiness of his new sandals, Long, with Duc's help, rubbed them vigorously with sand until the blood and history were gone.

Sometimes Long didn't wear shorts, especially during monsoon season when his body was wet even on days without any rain. Long and his brother Duc had no parents. Long weighed about thirty pounds, ribs visible, skinny at about five years old compared to Duc, who was bigger and darker at nearly seven. Villagers nicknamed them: Long, "White Peanut" and Duc, "Black Peanut." Families shared food with the boys, rice being a staple.

Like dogs with no home, Long had his favorite people, like Ba Phuong. Kids called older women "Ba" out of respect. Phuong means "Phoenix," a bird of beauty. In mythology, the Phoenix rose, coming back to life, time and again. She always had a smile for Long and Duc and gave them rice as often as they wanted. Inhaling the scent of the warm grains in the small bowl made this a cherished ritual for the boys, especially when offered by Ba Phuong. Pretty, with long black hair, kind eyes, and a ready smile, she gave Long and Duc hugs whenever they appeared.

"Good morning, Long and Duc! How are you boys doing today? I just made some rice. Would you like some?" When she put her arms around him, Long felt safe, wanted, not alone. The boys sat cross-legged for hours, told Ba Phuong about their day at Flower Bridge.

"Duc made the biggest splash ever today. It almost reached the bottom of the bridge!" bragged Long. "I want to jump off the bridge when I'm bigger, but I don't want to now," he continued.

Most of the children in the village did not know their parents, their creation often a result of casual encounters between village women and American or Vietnamese soldiers—in other cases, a byproduct of the women selling their bodies. During the war, prostitution became necessary and lucrative for many women. No one thought less of them for that, survival being paramount.

Long noticed how his brother's skin wasn't the same as his own: "Duc looks different than me, dark skin like some of the American soldiers. That's ok, we are brothers," he would declare.

Little girls liked Duc, outgoing and always taking risks, the first off the bridge, first to climb the impossible tree, a teaser. He chased the little girls, hid behind trees to scare them, jumped out making them squeal, delighted. He leapt out with a big growl and smiling eyes that said I'm your friend.

Long though stayed quiet, shy, an observer. *I don't know what to say to the other kids, so I let Duc talk for me.* Engaging with others challenged Long. If someone approached first, okay, but he didn't dare approach others first, like a shy puppy. Long the observer watched everything: always taking in how things worked, how people interacted, how rice is made, how huts are built. He tried to figure out why the soldiers had to always be there, why all the smoke and rockets, and what they were fighting about. *Why are they fighting? I don't understand. They're people, and we're people.*

Frustrated, Long tried to figure out why they had to fight. "I never want to become a soldier. It doesn't make sense," he told Duc. Maybe fathers and grandfathers knew the reason, but Long and Duc didn't have a father or a grandfather. Why would they take away twelve-year-old boys, never to be seen again?

CHAPTER 3
------------------------

# THE WAR IS HERE

I t is the first of the year, 1975. The PAVN (People's Army of Vietnam), the "North Vietnamese," had fought their way to less than 75 miles from Saigon. Public pressure in the United States had paved the way for a withdrawal of troops from Vietnam, which left the country vulnerable, defeat certain. Years of suffering, loss of thousands of US and Vietnamese lives, unthinkable horror and loss would soon be over.

This war had no good outcome. Fear of communism's spread, the adult boogeyman of the twentieth century, led to its start. "Let one country fall to communism, and the rest will fall with it." 58,000 US lives lost—those 58,000 families coping with death didn't necessarily subscribe to that notion, but they suffered the ultimate loss. The death toll of locals in Vietnam climbed even higher—2 million civilians, 1.1 million North Vietnamese and Viet Cong fighters, and 250,000 South Vietnamese soldiers perished in the conflict. Egotistical and self-righteous imposition of democracy, ultimately failing, had its price.

**Communists Take Over Saigon; U.S. Rescue Fleet Is Picking Up Vietnamese Who Fled in Boats**

'HO CHI MINH CITY'

Communications Cut Soon After Raising
of Victory Flag

By George Esper
The Associated Press

**Saigon, South Vietnam, April 30, 1975** - Communist troops of North Vietnam and the Provisional Revolutionary Government of South Vietnam poured into Saigon today as a century of Western influences came to an end.

Scores of North Vietnamese tanks, armored vehicles and camouflaged Chinese built trucks rolled to the presidential palace.

The President of the former non-Communist Government of South Vietnam, Gen. Duong Van Minh, who had gone on radio and television to announce his administration's surrender, was taken to a microphone later by North Vietnamese soldiers for another announcement. He appealed to all Saigon troops to lay down their arms and was taken by the North Vietnamese soldiers to an undisclosed destination.

The transfer of power was symbolized by the raising of the flag of the National Liberation Front over the presidential palace at 12:15 P.M. today, about two hours after General Minh's surrender broadcast, symbolized the transfer of power.

**Hundreds in Saigon Cheer**

Hundreds of Saigon residents cheered and applauded as North Vietnamese military vehicles moved to the palace grounds from which the war against the Communists had been directed by President Nguyen Van Thieu, who resigned April 21, and by President Ngo Dinh Diem, killed in a coup in 1963.

Broadcasting today in the early hours of the Communist take-over, the Provisional Revolutionary Government's representatives said:

"We representatives of the liberation forces of Saigon formally proclaim that Saigon had been totally liberated. We accept the unconditional surrender of Gen. Duong Van Minh, President of the former Government."

ॐॐॐ

Long and Duc emerged from the water under the bridge and ran to the village to find Ba Phuong. She'd know what to do. But when they arrived at her hut, they didn't find her. "She's always here, where is she?" Long screamed, an octave higher than his usual calm tone.

Long took in the all the people scurrying in every direction to avoid the massive tanks, which appeared to have no one in them.

Duc called out, "let's go this way!" The boys didn't know where they were running to, but as the squealing of metal and grinding of gears grew, they kept on, afraid they'd be eaten by the no-wheeled monsters. They ran.

"Duc, my feet hurt; they're bleeding from the rocks. I'm too tired! I can't breathe." Though Duc could run faster, he never left Long behind. The running crowds grew larger, Duc grabbed Long's hand to be sure they wouldn't get separated. Both hands wet from sweating, they held on.

Jet planes soared above, loud and deafening. They ducked each time one roared over them. The closer the grinding noises sounded and the more exhausted they got, the faster they ran. Fear drove them to speeds neither ever imagined. They sprinted, leaving the only life they knew far behind them.

*Where are you, Ba Phuong? Please find us, you will know what to do,* Long prayed. More miles, more hours, more blood from the soles of their feet, dehydrated from sweating, they ran on, escaping screaming, terrifying vibrations, the flying rockets overhead.

The bright sun blinded them as it approached the horizon, and with the sunset, crowds thinned. Loud noise softened.

❧ ❧ ❧

Duc and Long grew wearier than they thought they could ever endure, without any idea where they were. They found a place with grass and trees, rested at last. Though they never belonged to anyone, they'd not experienced this kind of loneliness; they cried for village friends and, most of all, Ba Phuong.

"Long, I don't know where we are! I don't know the way back." They sat in silence, with no idea where to go. Long looked at Duc for answers as he always did, but he had none. On the cool grass, with the sun over the horizon, they fell asleep, exhausted.

Voices and commotion woke them. The crowds that ran yesterday now stood still, all looking confused. Long noticed the buildings around the grass. Stores, restaurants, vegetable stands all empty. The boys huddled together. Long, always the observer, noticed children gathering in the distance, beyond their green patch with trees, blocks down from the stores and stands.

Pointing to the children, Long said, "Let's get with them."

Duc nodded, and they scampered to the group of kids. Farther away, they saw trucks—soldier trucks. "I hope they have food and water," Duc said.

Both desert-thirsty and terribly hungry, they had no food, no water for over a day. The Vietnamese soldiers told the children to line up. The other soldiers nearby looked different, bigger, loading supplies, sweating, but with friendly faces. Long told Duc, "These soldiers look like good guys, must be American soldiers." Just then, a Vietnamese soldier called out orders to the children, sending them in different directions: "You line up for this truck. You line up for the second truck. You wait here." As Long and Duc's survival instincts kicked in, they stepped quietly into line behind the other children.

A soldier directed Long and Duc to get on the third of many trucks and sit on the benches along the side. Duc's toes just reached the truck floor; Long's feet dangled. They sat on the right side, facing the children sitting on the left. Waiting anxiously, they heard one of the soldiers, maybe the boss, yell out, "Start 'm up!"

The trucks roared, smoke pluming in the air, wafting the diesel smell everywhere. The first truck pulled away, then the second, then Long and Duc's truck. Theirs chugged forward, shifting gears. All the kids started laughing, so Long laughed too. Duc joined in the merriment as the vehicles lurched forward, faster and faster. They'd never been in a truck before, amazed at the dust-spray flying out the back. They watched everything, excited at the sense of adventure.

A canvas top came down the sides about a foot, leaving the remaining space down to the truck bed open. The sensation of air whooshing in their faces seemed like flying, just like they felt diving off Flower Bridge into the water. But this wind, cooling them and blowing their hair all over, did not stop. The truck bounded down the road, and with each big bump the children cheered, bouncing up and down in the air. Duc laughed; Long squealed with delight.

Long tried to gauge the position of the sun, where it shone, but he could not figure out where the truck took them or why. "Are we getting closer to home?" he whispered to his brother. Looking down the aisle in the center of the truck, Long thought about an escape route and whether they'd need one. He wondered where these soldiers—this truck—wanted to take them. No answer came.

Sleep creeped in and the children stopped looking around and talking when the daylight evaporated and the wind cooled. The lights in the front of the trucks now the only way they could see, theirs, and those of the trucks behind them. Duc's head nodded, he slept sitting up. Long felt a sense of calm, this had to be a good thing—this truck, the pleasant American soldiers. One soldier even smiled at him, ruffled his hair when they got on. The steady drone of the engines made Long sleepy; he fought to keep his eyes open but then laid his head on Duc's lap, and slept.

# CHAPTER 4

## THE PLANE

A soldier's voice broke through Long's sleep: "Everybody up! Get down from the truck! Line up here, single file!"

Groggy, Long grabbed Duc's hand and followed the other kids off the truck. Long shivered from the bitter cold, tried not to feel scared.

Uncertain, the boys moved forward, away from the trucks. They followed the other kids, rounding a corner. Then Long exclaimed, "Duc, look!" Before them stood a large carrier plane. "This airplane is huge!"

In a ragged line, a soldier led all the kids up the ramp and inside. Long had never seen anything this big. It was much bigger than the monster tanks with no wheels, but the same color green.

The kids in front of them followed the soldier up the stairs, turning left. The soldier told them to sit on the floor, stay close together so everyone could fit. All the kids squeezed in, Long and Duc huddled together. Through Long's thin shorts, he could feel the icy metal floor.

Duc said, "Wow, cold floor feels pretty good." It reminded him of those refreshing plunges he took each day into the cool water beneath Flower Bridge.

The kids quieted, stopping their squealing, laughing, crying. Then a sudden "bang" echoed through the plane, causing Long to jump, startled. Duc craned his neck, trying to follow the source of the sound, which seemed to be just on the other side of the door, shut tight by the soldiers. *They'd never be able to escape if they had to, Long* thought, dejected. Moments later, a loud roar elicited crying from some of the kids as lights flashed on and the plane moved—first slowly, then so fast Long thought they'd die for sure.

Then it was only hushed sound. Feeling the vibration of the floor, Duc reassured Long, "Long, can you feel this? We're up in the air…we're flying into the sky!"

Long felt his heart beat hard, inside his chest a thrill buzzed. After the bumpy truck, this felt nice, cold but nice. He cuddled up to Duc and slept.

"Okay kids, wake up for your C-Rats." A soldier with red-colored hair, handed each kid a little box. Long's belly growled loudly.

Duc said, "Long, open the package, it's food—we get to eat! These soldiers give us food!"

In the C-Rats box, they found cans with an opener, toilet paper, cigarettes, matches, and white candy shaped like an "O." In a box given to them that looked like a miniature train car, they found crackers.

"Don't eat everything in the box, save some in case we get hungry later." Duc said.

He and Long ate from the cans with little spoons after watching some of the bigger kids, saved the candy, and ate a few of the crackers.

"Hey you kids, you parlay English?" one of the American soldiers said. "No? Well, this guy here," he pointed to a Vietnamese soldier, "is gonna tell you what I'm saying in your own language. This here plane we call a C 130 cargo plane. We're flying you to Malaysia, you savvy?"

From the floor, Long mirrored Duc, smiling when Duc smiled, laughing when Duc laughed. Other soldiers sat on benches lining each side of the plane. The kids were all busy eating and listening to the Vietnamese soldier tell them what the red-haired soldier said.

The soldiers looked tired, dirty—their faces streaked with sweat, or maybe tear tracks. Some had blood on their clothes. Some stared straight ahead too exhausted to sleep; others slept sitting up. Each contemplated their time in war, the horrors they'd seen or perpetrated, hoping to erase these memories forever and get back home.

Their bellies full with C-Rats and Coca-Cola, all the kids shrieked loudly when the plane wheels touched down with a massive bounce. "Is the monster plane angry?" Long asked Duc. Before he could answer, they felt the plane try to stop, surge forward, then backward, as the frightened kids screamed. Long held on to his little box of food.

The boss soldier shouted: "Get on your feet, line up. We're gettin' off the plane. When you get outside, line up, then sit your behinds on the pavement."

It was dark outside, only the lights of planes flying overhead. The boys sat on the ground for a long time, not talking, not laughing. All quiet. Long whispered to Duc, "What's gonna happen? This ground hurts my butt."

No one knew where they were or what was going to happen to them. But all the kids stayed put, the older ones, the little ones. All remained quiet, some sleeping, some staring at the sky or the soldiers who stayed with them, talking to each other.

The sun rose—a direction Long knew was always east—warming their bare legs, their cold feet. They lined up, getting behind a soldier who kept motioning them to follow him. They walked and walked, around big buildings, until they came upon a silver airplane shining in the sun, seeming even bigger than the green one. It had wings longer than the bridge Long never got to jump off. So beautiful, its silver body glimmered. An American soldier read the red, white and blue lettering emblazoned on side of the plane: *American Airlines.*

"Long, look, look, we're going to fly again in that big shiny plane," Duc said excitedly.

One by one, each kid climbed the silver metal stairs to board and were immediately left slack-jawed by the rows of big, soft chairs. Would they each have their own or would they have to sit on the floor again? The floors had rugs all over them.

Beautiful ladies wore clothes that looked like the women in magazines Long once saw, with pink cheeks and red lips. One lady, who smelled so good, gently picked up Long from beneath his armpits and placed him into one of the soft seats; Duc climbed into the seat next to him. They held hands tightly. The lady pulled out two belts and attached them together over their bellies, buckling them in. Everything smelled good: the plane, the air—so clean. Beautiful women making sure everything's OK, wearing uniforms like soldiers but more colorful.

*Pretty, but Ba pretty too. I hope she's ok,* thought Long.

## CHAPTER 5

---

# AMERICA

The plane taxied to the runway, hesitated, then took its position for takeoff. The engines revved to maximum, and the brakes released; Long and Duc held on while being pushed back into their seats with the force of the plane gaining speed, lifting its nose, and entering takeoff attitude. The boys leaned over to the window to watch the trees, buildings, and ground disappear. They could see out of this plane, unlike the freezing cargo plane. Long and Duc looked at each other giddy as the plane angled right, pointing to the United States.

"It's all blue now, the sky and below!" Long marveled.

As they settled in their comfortable seats, Long thought back to the times he and Duc sat on the ripped abandoned couches in the village, just contemplating. When the plane settled into its flight pattern, the beautiful ladies came around and offered them drinks and some peanuts. With big smiles, the boys happily accepted this offering, devouring the peanuts and Coca-Cola.

After a short nap, the ladies came by again, this time with more wonderful food!

The stewardess showed them how to drop their tray tables, and then put the warm meal in front of them. The boys broke apart the never-before-seen hamburgers and ate the meat and bread in pieces. Alongside the burgers were French fries, also new to the boys, which they devoured with relish and smiles bigger than those produced by the tasty hamburgers. After polishing off every morsel on their trays, they were offered vanilla ice cream with chocolate sauce. The stewardess showed them how to use the spoons. Long and Duc were so happy with this special treat, they displayed their joy by painting chocolate and vanilla moustaches on themselves. They couldn't stop pointing and laughing at one another and their good fortune.

"Yes, we are going to like America!" Duc declared.

After their good food and merriment, the boys flipped through the magazines in the seat pocket in front of them, but with full bellies and soft seats soon fell asleep.

"I think we are going back to the ground," Duc observed as the engines quieted. The plane turned to the right and again to the right, and as the ground came closer, Long said, "This must be America!"

With a modest bump, the boys looked out the chocolate moustache-smudged window to see their new place—to see America. Once stopped, they saw green trucks with canvas tops like the ones they rode in 7,000 miles ago. But it was all quiet here with no jets in the sky…no gunfire, no smoke. It was night, and all they could see were the trucks under lights and darkness beyond that. The air was different; it did not make them wet without rain. It smelled different—not bad, not good—just different.

*What will America be like?* Long wondered.

From below the stairs, a soldier shouted. Pointing, he told the children to form lines and load into the green trucks. They could not understand, but the gestures were clear. They followed some of the older kids who seemed to know what they were doing. Long and Duc always stayed together, Duc being sure his little brother was safe. Up the ramp and into the trucks, it was just like the ones they rode in at home: canvas tops, open air. But they were cleaner and newer, not muddy and dusty. They bounced along, but unlike their trip in Vietnam, there was no laughter about the wind gusting in their faces or the bouncing of the vehicle driving over the pitted road. Uncertainty was on the little faces in the back of the truck.

## First Night

The trucks stopped at a pleasant-looking place. The boys did not know what kind of place it was but saw the palm trees, parked cars, swimming pool, bright pink and blue sign, and a building with lots of windows surrounding rows of colorful doors. They overheard the truck driver saying the word "motel," so they assumed the place's name: *Motel.* The children were given rooms and told with gestures to stay in them. Upon entering their room, Long and Duc saw two beds, a separate room with a toilet, and something they'd never seen before—a bathtub that they thought to be a small swimming pool.

"This is going to be fun! Let's go swimming," Duc suggested happily.

After playing with the knobs, the boys figured out how to make the water come out to fill the bathtub. When one knob was turned and the shower came on, drenching them, they couldn't hold back the laughter. They hopped into the tub and splashed water all over the place, frolicking noisily, and having the most amazing time.

America!

They heard a loud knock on the door—it opened fast, and a soldier looked at them sternly with his finger over his mouth. The soldier's expression might have been forbidding, but his eyes were laughing. Long and Duc got the message—pipe down. After they dried off with the clean towels, they tried the soft beds with pillows: amazing and so much better than a mat on the ground. There were two beds, but they slept together in one of them.

Early in the morning, before the sun came up, back on the trucks they all went. In about half the time it took for their ride in Vietnam, they arrived at a place with many buildings, all with sharp edges, square with countless windows, all alike. Like the trucks, everything looked clean. Still night, yellow-haze lights on top of tall poles lit the area. The boys fixed their gazes on the moths flying around the lights. The trucks stopped. Loud engines now silenced, a soldier waved the children down the ramp and told them to sit on the ground. No one spoke.

As the sun came up, the boss soldier barked, "Stand up and form lines."

Standing, they saw the sun glowing over the hilltops, first orange, then yellow, then white. The sky turned from black to cloudless blue. When Long and Duc turned the other way, they saw the big blue ocean. Beautiful. Looking around again, they spotted very few green trees, no green jungle, only brown bushes that had tiny flowers on them scattered over the small hills for miles.

Getting used to the ways of the Americans now, the regimentation comforted them. The children marched in lines around the buildings to a massive tent, and inside Long saw rows and rows of beds. There were no walls other than the outside ones, with bright lights above and poles holding up the top of the tent. The soldiers pointed to the beds, and Long understood they should each sit on one.

"Duc, we get our own beds! Let's choose the ones by the wall, OK?"

This tent and these beds would be their home for what turned out to be more than a year.

**New Home**

The soldiers gave the children birthdays based on how old they looked. They also gave them American names. "Duc" sounded like "Duke," so that became his American name. They gave Long the name Tom, but looking down at the floor, arms folded and shaking his head, Long refused. "I don't want that name. I want my own name."

Long had seen Tom and Jerry cartoons and didn't want the name of a cat; so, he insisted, and they allowed him to keep "Long" as his name. As for his brother, he knew Duc got a kick out of his American name, but for Long, there was no "Duke," only Duc.

The boys learned that the place they stayed had a name also, Camp Pendleton. Long and Duke and all the other kids were assigned a person called a mentor who played with them, taught them some English, and spent time with them to make them feel at home and learn to blend into American society.

When the mentors left, they played with the other kids. Long's mentor-soldier, named Jim, drove a truck and took Long on rides with him. "Hey Duc, I'm riding in the front! Not in the back like before."

Long watched Jim start the truck with a button, shift into gear with his foot on the brake, and push on the accelerator until the truck lurched forward. Long examined the controls Jim used—when Jim braked, when Jim shifted—and got the hang of how to operate a truck. He stretched his neck to see the scenery and hoped that he would grow faster so he could see out without stretching.

After a few rides, Jim put Long on his lap and let him steer the massive truck, careful to keep one knee pressed on the wheel. "OK, Long, hold your hands on the wheel like this, and I'll handle the speed. Keep looking at the road in front of ya and way out there, so ya know what's comin."

Long concentrated on his mission, pointing the truck between the lines on the road, careful not to veer off. Long felt important, got a bit cocky even when he jumped off the truck after "driving." He felt taller. After the drive, Jim gave Long a piece of candy as a reward for his driving prowess. Long ran and found Duc to report, "I drove the truck! I steered it and kept it on the road. It was so fun!"

Duc beamed a proud grin to Long, his forever brother.

Duke's soldier, a small, stocky, muscular man named Roberto, had rank. Strong and powerful, Roberto was nicknamed "Emperor" by the boys because soldiers would get in line when he raised his voice. Long realized that Duc always had someone more important, like getting the high-ranking soldier instead of a truck driver. Roberto gave Duke whole bags of candy. *Duc was the lucky one, the extrovert, the better-looking one.* Long, the introvert, the observer, the smaller, got less. But this did not ruffle Long who thought, *I don't mind that Duc gets more. He's bigger, stronger, and my older brother. He should get better.*

❧❧❧

The boys stayed at Camp Pendleton for what felt a long time to them. Seasons passed, with Long offered a jacket because the weather got cold, but later felt too hot to wear. Duke, whose mentor was Roberto the Emperor, got a nicer jacket than Long. Long noticed but did not mind.

At Camp Pendleton, the children had no responsibilities, no schooling or classes of any kind. They learned a little English listening to their mentors and to the soldiers that handed them food at mealtimes. They played all day—lined up for breakfast, then played, lined up for lunch, then played, lined up for dinner, then lights out. Camp Pendleton looked so huge to them, with miles of open, shrub-covered hills and fields and the occasional dirt road, where the trucks and tanks passed during military maneuvers. The boys were not allowed in those areas but managed to get a glimpse anyway.

During one of their wanderings, the boys found an unexpected treasure trove of toys inside a small building. The boys were allowed to check out a few to bring back to their tent-home. Long picked Mighty Mouse and also a toy military truck that looked like the one he "drove" so well with Jim. After many visits to the toy building, one day they came to find all the doors locked—no toys. *Where did they go?* Long wondered.

The number of children brought to Camp Pendleton had been decreasing slowly over the year and as children were placed in foster homes or adopted, outside support for them had been decreasing as well. With resources tightening, military management decided to end the "Toys for Loan" store.

On one of their night explorations, Long and Duc wandered off and found a building where they showed movies. The boys watched Mighty Mouse and the Lone Ranger. Afterwards, Long chattered excitedly, "Mighty

Mouse's amazing, with his muscles and flying, always saving people from trouble!"

What a noble mouse, that Mighty Mouse. Long didn't understand the Lone Ranger: "Why does he wear a mask over his eyes? Why does Tonto say only a word here and a word there—like a grunt?"

Long related to Tonto, trying to communicate but not having the words to say what he meant. "Maybe we can meet the Lone Ranger and Tonto," Long said to Duc.

They appeared to ride their horses in the same kind of dry desert area where he and Duc lived, open land with not many buildings. The boys kept coming back to the movie area, but then one day that, too, disappeared. No one cared what the kids did. They had no adult supervision—they got fed, and beyond that, were on their own. No one told them to shower, brush their teeth, or change clothes.

Beyond their area of Camp Pendleton, they could see a hill, with trails like mountain bike trails. At the top of the hill, they could see a giant cross and a restaurant which had a huge yellow sign on top, large windows all around and plants below them, lined up like the soldiers, with parking places in front where several cars parked. The boys climbed over the ridge to it, and from outside watched the TVs in the restaurant, which were always playing *Star Trek*.

Long watched people go into the restaurant, get seated, have food served to them by ladies that reminded Long of the pretty women on the shiny airplane. Families with moms and dads and children came and went. Long wondered what it would be like to live in an American family. They'd never known families like this in the village where they grew up. The whole village felt like a family.

From the top of the hill, Long could see cars but not the ocean. He started to forget memories of his village: the people, the bridge, the splashes, the tanks, and Ba Phuong. He wanted to get to know his new home, so he explored every day to see what he could, what the place had to offer. When soldiers caught him near the restaurant, they told him to go back down to the non-restricted area. So, he figured out how to get around without anyone seeing him. Long the Observer wanted to know how American families lived, and also to watch *Star Trek* from outside the restaurant.

## CHAPTER 6

---

# BA PHUONG

Carefully cooking rice like most days, Ba Phuong noticed the noise felt louder. The ground vibrated, exhibited in her pot of rice that now seemed to stir itself. When a rocket landed feet from where she cooked, panic electrified her.

Ba ran next door to her dear friend Ba Han for comfort and direction. She saw rice heating on the fire there also, with even more ripples in the pot, but no Ba Han. Stepping back outside, Ba looked around the village, which appeared ghostly in the smoke, with most of the people gone and those remaining paralyzed in fear staring out into the streets.

"I have to find the boys! They must be down by Flower Bridge," Ba yelled out loud to no one in particular. With jets overhead, she ran towards the now approaching tanks in the direction of Flower Bridge. *The boys will be frightened—I must get there to help them.*

She was the only person running in that direction. All others were running away from the noise and tanks, but she had to find her precious boys. Ba did not have her own children, but Long and Duc were close to it. She fed them and comforted them almost every day and listened to their conquests on Flower Bridge and around the village.

In a cloud of awful smelling smoke, Ba saw the outline of Flower Bridge. The tanks were not yet there, but moving towards it quickly. She kept to the side and tried to be as invisible as possible as she approached the bridge. She got there, stood at the edge, where the boys had jumped to compete for the biggest splash, and saw no one. She looked down at the bushes cloaking the hill below and the well-worn path used by the kids post-splash. No children. She ran to the other side of the bridge, looked underneath for little ones hiding. No children.

*Where did they go?*

More tanks came as jets banked down. Rockets exploded beyond the smoke fog. She ran back toward the village. *Where next?* The village was empty—the black, putrid smoke quieting the village from the approaching doom. She threw some clothes in a bag and ran. Still young, she caught up easily with others running in the same direction, their faces stretched with fear. The old walked as fast as possible, the young running past them. As Ba ran, she scanned for the boys, sometimes calling out their names to boys that looked similar in the distance.

*I wish I thought to bring water*, regretted Ba, her mouth dusty from the smoke and kick-up of other runners. She pressed ahead.

As the sun dropped, the noise subsided. People were not running anymore. The tanks and planes must have done their work.

She stopped along with many of the others in a small, unknown village, where shops naked of inventory surrounded a small park. People wandered past locked storefronts or sat next to vegetable stands, left empty.

Ba found a grassy area where she could stop. She leaned up against a tree that wasn't occupied, lost in her confusion about what to do next.

*Where are Long and Duc?*

She sat to think but soon fell asleep.

Eventually, the sun pulled her from her weary sleep. People still lingered, not knowing what to do or where to go. In the distance, past the village, she saw soldiers and lines of Army trucks. Around the vehicles were children along with Vietnamese and American soldiers. Ba ran through the village towards the trucks, excited that Long and Duc

BRUCE CARLIN

might be there. However, a perimeter fence separated the soldiers and children from others. Ba Phuong peeked through the fence, straining to find the boys. Children were lining up and climbing into the trucks. "I can't see them!" Ba muttered out loud.

She tried to get through the entrance but was held back. "This is a rescue operation for the children. No one else. Command orders," said the soldier at the gate.

She craned her neck to see around him to locate the boys, but there were too many.

The trucks pulled away, their engines loud as they moved through the gears.

ॐॐॐ

Back in the village, the war ended. In a day, the country transformed from war zone to unfamiliar calm. Ba's heart empty over not finding her dear boys, she walked back the miles she had run a day ago. Villagers returned, and life became normal again, but without the soldiers and noise—and without Long and Duc.

**The Man from Hong Kong**

After many years of heartache, Ba eventually settled into her life without the boys. Her pulse still raced on seeing young ones who reminded her of Duc and Long, but she chided herself. *They are grown now. I'll never see them again.* One day as Ba Phuong shopped for supplies in town, she reached for a new rice pot and her eyes met Danh's. He smiled politely and said "hello" in Vietnamese. He appeared different, dressed better than the men in the area. She replied "hello" and smiled back. Shy, Ba went about her shopping. Danh circled around, also shy, but captured by Phuong's smile, he timidly asked, "Would you like to join me for some tea?"

Without hesitation, she replied "yes" in her native dialect, feeling somehow comfortable with the man. Her instinct said to trust him.

Supplies in hand, they walked together to a nearby tea and coffee place. Ba Phuong smiled inside. This handsome stranger felt genuine.

"I'm from Hong Kong. I grew up here but moved to Hong Kong for a job opportunity at HSBC Bank. Hong Kong is a beautiful place, like here but with skyscrapers, bright lights, and many, many people. I miss the quiet of Vietnam, but really enjoy the excitement of Hong Kong. Do you live nearby?" Danh asked.

"Yes, in the village about a mile from here. Things are changing so fast here since the end of the war."

"Do you have family here?" he asked.

"I did, two boys, not actually mine, but they were like my own. At the end of the war, in all the chaos, I lost them. I hope they are ok…" Ba fell into silence for a moment as worry crept once again into her expression. Then continued, "I think they might have gone with the American soldiers when Saigon fell."

"I am so sorry. That must have been terrible. What are their names?"

A soft smile curved Ba's lips as she spoke of her beloved boys: "Long and Duc. We called them "white peanut" and "black peanut" in the village—they were nothing alike. Duc was crazy, outgoing, always joking, jumping out of trees, teasing the girls. Long was smart, pensive… gentle. So different, but they never left each other's sides. I loved them…still…love." Ba's Vietnamese faltered just a bit, her emotion taking over.

"Have you tried to find them?"

"I did for a time, but no one could tell me anything. There was such chaos at the end of Saigon. There was no order, no leadership, everyone trying to stay alive and protect their families and belongings."

Two hours later, they each finished their third cup of tea.

"I visit here every few months for business. I would love to see you again," said Danh.

"I would love to see you also!"

They politely hugged, and Danh walked off.

When out of sight, Phuong skipped like a little girl back to the village. She felt smile-tears filling her eyes. She decided to stop and buy some makeup.

In less than a month, Danh called. "I'll be in Vietnam next week. I would love to see you again."

Trying to keep from squeaking, she said, "Absolutely! I would love to see you also!"

Over dinner, they could not stop talking, both so excited at having found each other. Afterward, they took a walk in the always-warm, humid evening. He grabbed her hand. A flush spread through her body. After walking and window-shopping for hours, Danh said, "I have meetings early in the morning and need to be fresh. Could we have dinner again tomorrow?"

"Yes, of course!"

He walked her home, gave her a small kiss on the cheek, and left for his hotel. Danh hoped he hadn't blown it with Ba by cutting the date short. He was uncomfortable with his relationship skills, at least when it came to love.

Danh took a shortcut back to his hotel. He needed some sleep, though it didn't come easily with his excitement about his growing relationship with Phuong. The streets were dark in that part of town, and Danh picked up his walking pace. He scanned ahead and to the side; the light was scarce. His unease was suddenly met with excruciating pain, a bright flash in his head, then nothing.

The police found him lying on the street, blood pouring from the wound on his head. The pocket from his pants was pulled inside-out where his wallet normally resided.

Three days later, he awoke with blurred vision in the hospital. His head ached worse than any migraine he had ever experienced. He asked the nurse, "What happened to me?"

Mr. Nguyen, you were brought here by the police. Apparently, you were mugged."

"What day is it?"

"It's Thursday," said the nurse.

"Oh my god! I saw Phuong on Monday!"

ఈఈఈ

Ba Phuong carefully worked on her new makeup for her next dinner with Danh. It took her three times to get the lipstick on right, without it bleeding over. A little eye liner worked fine, she told herself as she observed the unfamiliar person she saw in the mirror. Excited, she now felt ready. It was almost six, and Danh was a very punctual gentleman.

She sat by the door, waiting for the knock.

Then it was seven, then eight. *What happened? Surely, he would call if he was late or was still in his meetings!*

Tuesday came.

Then Wednesday. Phuong kept asking herself if she said something wrong. *Should I have invited him in?*

It didn't make sense. She knew how they both felt about each other.

*What happened?*

Thursday morning, the phone rang.

"Hello!" Phuong answered.

"This is Nurse Ha from Tran Hung Dao Hospital. Is this Phuong?"

"Yes."

"Danh Nguyen is here and asked that I call you. I'm afraid he was injured Monday night and just woke up from a coma. He will get better, but right now it is difficult for him to speak."

"Oh no! How did it happen? I am coming there now." Ba's mind was racing with worry. She nearly hung up the phone before the nurse could reply.

"You can see him but just for a few minutes. He's in a lot of pain."

Grateful for the nurse's call, Ba quickly thanked her, hung up, and immediately packed a bag.

༨༨༨

Danh was ecstatic to see Phuong. His broad smile stretched his stitches, and he winced with pain. Ba ran over to his bed, hugging him gingerly. Danh loved the smell of her hair as she held on to him.

"How are you feeling, Danh?" Ba asked softly.

"I'm sorry I missed our dinner. I feel terrible about that," Danh said, neck tight as he glanced away with embarrassment.

"What happened?"

"The police said that I was mugged, hit on the head, knocked out, my wallet and watch stolen."

She held his hand, looking into his swollen eyes, careful not to tear up. She had to be strong for him.

"As soon as I can, I still want to have dinner with you. I can't right now because I get dizzy when I stand up."

Phuong giggled, then laughed as she hugged him, loving his humility and politeness. He was more concerned with missing their dinner than his own life-threatening situation. She was relieved that she had not done something wrong in his eyes.

After his recovery and a year's worth of every-few-months visits and dinners, Danh asked Phuong to marry him and move with him to Hong Kong.

## CHAPTER 7

---

# SEASON TWO.
# LEAVING CAMP PENDLETON

Long and Duke were playing not far from their bunk when a soldier approached them and instructed, "Come with me."

They looked at each other. Then Long asked Duc, "What do they want?"

"I don't know," replied Duc. *Long always thinks I have answers because I'm bigger and older, but I don't know... I just don't know,* thought Duc.

The soldier took them to their beds in the tent-home and told them to gather their belongings. They packed up their few things in a canvas bag Long found out in the field and followed the soldier to a car with wooden sides parked in the lot outside.

"Boys, this here is Fred. You're goin' with him to a new home."

Fred, a tall, thin man with a friendly, wrinkled face, and trimmed moustache, wore a fedora hat tilted to one side, baggy slacks and plaid shirt. Fred pointed to the rear of the car.

"Boys, put your things in the back of the wagon and get in the seat behind me."

Long's skills of observation were on high alert as they drove away from their year-long Camp Pendleton home to somewhere new. Long looked straight ahead, but his eyes scanned like searchlights. Duke, always restless, was looking around everywhere, cocking his head and trying to see as much as possible. "He seems nice, but I wish I knew where we're going," Long whispered to Duc.

They drove through mountains to the east, away from the ocean. Long pointed to a tunnel they approached which pierced the mountain – where sunlight and desert-like terrain gave way to a black hole with a wink of light at the end. Cars going in the other direction honked their horns to hear the echoes.

"How great is America, to have tunnels like *this*? How many men did it take to dig this giant hole in the mountain?" Long pondered aloud.

Miles later, they pulled off the road to a restaurant. It looked like the one where Long watched *Star Trek* through the windows and observed families coming and going. Now he sat *inside* such a restaurant for the first time. He often wondered, when spying on families in the diner from the mountain top, what it would be like to eat there—the painted face women bringing them food and smiling like the ladies on the big airplane.

Once inside, Fred flicked his hand toward the counter letting Long and Duke know to sit there, then he ordered food for them. The boys still did not speak much English, but had quickly learned the "survival triad": *nod, smile, and be polite*. To avoid confrontation, one should listen and be pleasant. When in doubt *nod, smile, and be polite*. The pretty waitress, mostly friendly, brought them hamburgers with French fries. Long ate hamburgers and fries before at Camp Pendleton, but how nice having the food handed to him with a smile.

When finished, they piled back into the wood-paneled station wagon, satisfied, but still anxious about where they'd end up. The day consisted of more miles, not much talk, and exhaustive scanning.

### The Old Lady's House

Fred parked in front of a typical suburban American home. An older woman was at the door.

"Boys, this here is Mrs. Ketchum. She will take care of you for a while. Grab yer bag and go with her."

The small, hunched-over woman, Sarah Ketchum—neat and clean in a floral dress, sneakers, and her hair back in a bun—met the boys, extending a shaky hand. "Long and Duke, welcome to my house."

The 1950's musty tract home had sparse plantings in front and needed new paint. Mrs. Ketchum showed Long and Duke to their room, a small and dark place with two twin beds covered by floral bedspreads. The place smelled old. Mrs. Ketchum said with a stern smile, "This will be your room. Please keep it neat so I don't have to clean up after you."

The next morning, Ms. Ketchum gave Long and Duke their first ever bowl of cereal with milk. In Vietnam, they drank only water, drawn with a scoop from a rain-catching vessel, never milk. They liked the cereal a lot, so good! The boys gave an extra-exuberant *nod, smile, and be polite.*

Ms. Ketchum took them with her wherever she went because they could not be left alone. Her old, foul-smelling car was kept in a separate building in her back yard. Each time the boys accompanied her, Long opened the back window, trying to put his head out, and often had to hold back the urge to throw-up from the movement and smell until the old lady stopped the car. One time, Long did vomit inside the car because he couldn't get fresh air. Ms. Ketchum got upset by this but cleaned up the mess.

They went to church every Sunday and attended bible school, where Long was interested in what they had to say. He tried to understand, but Long the Observer grew into a "show me" child, and increasingly, he found religion difficult to absorb. Faith in the invisible did not come easy to Long—the next meal and a safe place to sleep were far more important to him.

It wasn't long before the boys heard the familiar sound of Fred's station wagon, its noisy exhaust and squeaking brakes signaled his return. Long and Duke neither expected to see Fred again nor that he'd be taking them to another family. But since leaving Vietnam, they realized their survival depended on accepting what came. They'd spent fewer than two months with Sarah Ketchum.

"Afternoon, Sarah. Are the boys ready?" She hugged Long and Duke, wishing them well. *It smelled there, but I liked her. I'll miss her,* thought Long.

Waving goodbye, Long and Duke hopped into Fred's now familiar wood-sided station wagon and were driven for less than an hour before being dropped at their next family.

**Mrs. Lopez**

Fred introduced the boys to Mrs. Lopez and her family. "Mrs. Lopez, please meet Long and Duke! They're fine boys, well-behaved, and got good marks from their last family."

The boys bowed slightly and shook Mrs. Lopez's hand as she greeted them, "Please come in, boys."

Once the noise from Fred's smoky wagon faded, Mrs. Lopez sat the boys down in the living room. It was sparse and neat, didn't smell like the last house.

"Long and Duke, I have very strict rules here. I don't want you to sit on the chairs in the living room, and you must walk only on the plastic runner in the hall." The boys moved from the chairs and sat on the floor, cross-legged, eyes glued to Mrs. Lopez's.

"I only want you to be in your room. Use the bathroom when you need to, but don't mess it up."

The boys nodded and went to their room after Mrs. Lopez pointed to it. At dinner time, Mrs. Lopez brought beans in two small bowls to the boys. They got the same for breakfast, the same for lunch, all in their room, not at the dinner table. This would be their life at Mrs. Lopez's house: beans for breakfast, lunch, and dinner, in their room—prison without bars.

"We live here because this family gets extra money," Duc proclaimed to Long after a few days. "I heard Mrs. Lopez tell her friend on the phone that she gets money every month for having us here. I thought she did it cuz she's nice, but she doesn't care about us!" Duc, the normally energetic, curious, friendly boy, felt angry. "I feel like we are in a cage."

The only apparent bright spot was Elena Lopez's teenage daughter Gabriella, who spoke to the boys and acted nice to them. Long reasoned that she felt sorry for their one-room existence. One day Gabriella waved them out of the house when her mom left. They followed her to the park, taking twice as many steps to keep up. Long and Duke felt so excited to get out of the prison house—feel the sun, smell the grass.

At the park, Gabriella instructed them to sit on the bench and not move: "Don't play on the swings or anything else at the playground. Just sit here."

Once the boys were planted on the bench, Gabriella met her boyfriend and together went behind some trees where they kissed and did other things, making odd noises. The boys, sat quietly, looking forward, but moved their attention to the moaning behind the trees. A learning experience for Long and Duke—in America, boys and girls did those things.

A month later, they were picked up once again by Fred in his paneled wagon. "Mornin' boys. Here we go again. All packed?"

"Yes, we are!" proclaimed Long. The boys were excited to get out of their one-room, plastic-runner existence. Fred drove them far out into the country this time.

## The Wilsons

Their new home—the Wilsons'—quickly distinguished itself from their previous stays in American homes. On their introductory tour, in the backyard of the Wilson house, the boys spotted chicken coops.

"I will show you how to gather eggs, and each day I want you boys to gather eggs and bring them into the house," Mrs. Wilson explained. Long thought *this is great. We'll have something to do and not just sit in our room like last time.* They were shown their room: simple, two beds, but clean, with a closet.

The Wilson's boy, Gerald who was about the same age as Duke, had his own toy-filled room. Long and Duke knew they weren't allowed to go into Gerald's room or play with his toys. During their term there, they never played with Gerald, whom Long began calling "the spoiled kid"—to himself, of course.

One day, Long was gathering eggs in the chicken coop, while Gerald played in the back yard with a toy gun. Suddenly, as Long emerged from the coop, Gerald threw a large stick at Long, hitting him above the eye. In pain, Long cried, scared because of all the blood. Mrs. Wilson hearing the commotion, and noticing it was Long who was injured and not her son, impatiently strode out into the yard and whisked Long into the house.

Mrs. Wilson bandaged the shaking Long, while saying nothing to him. The spoiled kid never apologized nor did his parents make him. Long ignored Gerald even more the rest of the time there. Duke could not help the situation because the family ruled, and the boys counted for nothing.

A few months after the stick incident, Mrs. Wilson asked the boys, "Do you want to come with me to pick up Gerald?" They of course said yes, taking any opportunity to get out and see new things.

When Gerald climbed into the car, he immediately asked, "Can we get Slurpees?"

His mother nodded her head, smiling. Gerald, her prized son, got whatever he wanted. "Would you boys like one also?" she offered because she felt she had to. Delighted, Duke and Long accepted. Each Slurpee came with a lid that looked like a baseball cap, and the boys devoured theirs. "Another great American invention, fruit made into ice!" observed Long.

A few weeks later, Mr. Wilson stayed home during the day, which was unusual as he normally worked from early morning on at the tractor factory nearby. That day, there was a boat in the backyard sitting on a trailer hitched to his car.

"Boys, do you want to help me clean the boat?" Mr. Wilson asked.

Of course, they did—anything to get out of their room. The spoiled boy never helped with anything. After they cleaned the entire vessel, the boys watched as their foster parent picked up a fishing rod, another great American invention new to the boys.

Mr. Wilson called to Gerald, "Come on out to the boat, and let me show you somethin'."

He demonstrated for his son how to cast the fishing rod. Clumsy, Gerald gave a feigned attempt but did not have the desire nor the coordination to do it correctly. Impatient with his son, Mr. Wilson asked Long if he wanted to try casting the rod.

"Yes of course!" Long, a natural, cast the rod with a swift flick of the wrist into an imaginary lake.

"Great job!" proclaimed Mr. Wilson. Long responded with a shy smile. Long liked doing this, casting for a fish. *But it would be more fun in real water, not a backyard.*

Later, after the casting lesson, Mrs. Wilson told Long and Duke to pack their one suitcase with their belongings, while the family packed theirs. As instructed, they put their suitcase by the front door. Long and Duke looked at each other, excited, "We're going fishing on the boat! This will be the best adventure ever."

Waiting by the front door, Long and Duke wiggled their arms, standing on their toes, hopping around, anticipating their fishing expedition. Peering out through the screen door, they saw Fred drive up in his station wagon. He got out, hollering to the boys, "Get yer stuff and get in boys." From the backseat of Fred's wagon, they watched the Wilsons drive off, clean boat, fishing rods, and spoiled child in tow. Dismay and disappointment overwhelmed them. So excited to get out of their cell-like room, ride on a boat, and cast a fishing rod into real water, they didn't see it coming.

Long vowed to *never* trust any family again. Red-faced with anger and frustration, he yelled "We're just a paycheck to these people. They use us to do their work. They don't love us; they don't even like us. Why do we have to stay with these awful people!"

*america*.

**More New Families**

In the following years, Long and Duke moved from house to house, family to family, never trusting anyone. They station-wagoned with Fred from one home to the next, counting at least ten different homes over the years. Long never again opened himself up to disappointment. The families usually had kids, and often Long and Duc suffered slurs like *slant* or *chink*, all included in their rent-free existence. They had no other choice. Long knew that he and Duc represented a meal ticket for the family—a second job, with no emotional connection included in the bargain.

Families treated the boys with indifference, only paying attention to their own kids. At the Browns, where they stayed for several years, there was a boy named Bobby and a small girl named Joleen. Joleen, in potty training, used a porta potty. When unattended, Joleen liked to play with her poop; once, not long after the boys arrived, when Long walked by her room, Joleen chased him, holding her feces. Long crawled up on his bed where Joleen couldn't reach him.

The mother saw her daughter, smeared with feces trying to get to Long, and yelled at him for encouraging her daughter to use poop like clay. Every day at this house, Long and his brother had to pull weeds, clean up the trash, and sweep. They worked for their food and shelter, while Bobby and Joleen, the couple's biological children, got to stay in the house and play, never helping. Mrs. Brown made promises to the boys that if they pulled weeds in the yard they would get to go to the park, but Long and Duke never got to go—just another dangled reward that never came. This mother made the same kinds of promises to her own children but kept those promises.

One day when the boys were still living with the Browns, Long's teacher at his school in Simi Valley gave him a model car kit, which he took home and promptly put together with great care. He proudly put it on his night-stand to admire. But when he returned from school the following day, he found his model car shattered on the floor in his room.

Mrs. Brown told him unapologetically that her daughter broke it. She did not clean up the mess nor offer to replace it. Experience taught Long that he had no standing with the Browns—he was simply a commodity. The same thing happened with another of Long's scant possessions, a ceramic Japanese house, also discovered on the floor, broken.

Frustrated and angry, Long started putting his things on high shelves. Just as in other houses the boys stayed in, Long and Duke were always responsible for any chores— not their foster parents' children. When Long's frustration over the inequality became unbearable, he found himself yelling loudly, uncontrollably, at Mrs. Brown; it was the first time Long ever argued with anyone.

"We do all the work, the dishes, the trash, the weeding, and your kids do nothing!" Long protested. Mad to the point of tears, he went on, listing all the work he and Duke did. With the little English he knew, Long screamed at her in desperation.

Red-faced, Mrs. Brown smacked Long's head with an open hand, so hard he could not keep his balance and fell face down on the floor. In pain, he cried, then vowed he'd never give someone an excuse to lay a hand on him again. Long knew what he had to do, go back to the *nod, smile, and be polite* routine, only now Long felt a knot in his stomach from holding his rage in check.

Mrs. Brown never hit her own kids. She received money for keeping Long and his brother, while treating them like servants. Long and Duke would have been glad to help the family if only Mrs. Brown kept her promises and treated the boys like human beings.

## CHAPTER 8

---

# RUNAWAY

*I can't take this anymore. I won't do this anymore. Duc can handle this, but I can't.* Long packed a shirt, all his money from bottles collected and redeemed, plus money he had found, and left. He said nothing to his brother. He walked directionless, thinking. *Anything will be better than being a slave. I'll find something better.*

No destination in mind, he continued. The evening was cool. Long preferred shadows to the sunlight. Hours later, he saw a freeway ahead and decided to go there. When he reached Interstate 5, he stood at the south onramp under the streetlight with his thumb up. From the many trips in Fred's wagon, he had learned about hitch-hiking. He figured it was his only option to escape.

A guy in an old Chevy pickup pulled over and waved Long into his truck. Long ran up and got in, but kept his internal radar on. The driver met Long's eyes as he spoke plainly, "Yer kinda young to be hitch-hikin', 'specially at night."

"Uh, I look young, uh…yes. Thank you for picking me up." Still wary of people in general, Long kept his guard up, knowing politeness was his best defense.

"Where ya goin'?"

"Um, just this way is good, you can drop me when you get off the freeway."

The man's now short cigarette smelled terrible, even with the window open. Through the smoke, Long could make out the driver through his peripheral vision—a skinny, nice-enough looking guy wearing an old tee shirt and jeans. *Any weird move, I'll pull the handle and jump out*, Long thought. He was ready. But no need.

In Glendale, the man slowed his truck at the offramp. "This is where I get off. Where'd ya like me to drop you?"

"I'll get off here. Thank you very much for the ride."

"Yer welcome. You be good now!"

Long stood alone in the quiet night after his ride left, sounds of a few cars in the background. *What have I done? I've never been by myself. Where do I go from here?*

Upon returning home, the truck driver told his wife about picking up the little hitch hiker who was barely a teenager, if that. Having two small boys themselves, his wife chastised him, "You just dropped him off? You didn't offer to help him?"

"No, I thought he wouldn't want that."

"I'm going to call the police. A little boy like that shouldn't be running around at night alone!"

Long the Observer walked. It had been hours since he left—Long felt hunger but ignored it. He walked until he saw a Safeway supermarket, bright lights assaulting the dark night. He had money, mostly pennies and a few nickels, not enough to get food. He was terribly hungry. Though he hated his foster existence, he always had food.

He devised a plan which he knew wasn't right, but the hunger managed him. He went into the store, confident he could find something to eat that would fit under his shirt. He reasoned that he could grab some food and no one would suspect a kid. As he walked in, he noticed the lady policeman sitting in the cop car outside, but he wasn't concerned. Long paced an aisle of the store working up his courage, he noticed the lady officer was now inside, at the end of the aisle, looking directly at him. Long's heart raced. He hadn't taken any food yet but felt inexplicably guilty. He spotted an emergency exit at the back of the store and took off, running through the stockroom, past the restrooms, and out the emergency exit, setting off the alarm.

A young man and woman wearing tie-dyed Grateful Dead t-shirts, smoking pot in the back lot froze as the siren went off and a little boy bolted out the back door of the store. They watched as the police officer followed Long out and across the parking lot. Observing the chaos, the pot-smoking man stood up and yelled to Long, "Hey kid, come with me!"

Long ran toward the couple in tie-dye, sensing they were a better risk than the cop. Following the pair towards the unlit section of asphalt, Long stopped short at the 8 ft. fence defining the perimeter of the lot. The man reached down and grabbed Long by his beltloop, tossing him over the chain-link, then quickly scrambled over it himself, followed by his girlfriend. The three of them ran for several blocks, and when it was certain they had lost the cop, they stopped to catch their breath. Laughing from the excitement of running and still high from smoking weed, the man asked, "What's your name?"

"I'm Long. Thank you for helping me."

"I'm Tim. This is Ellie. We live a coupla blocks from here. Where you from?"

"Simi Valley. I live in a foster family house. I couldn't stand it anymore, so I left."

"You don't have a place to live?"

"No."

Ellie glanced at Tim with an *awe he's cute* expression and said, "You can stay with us for a while if you want."

"Yes, I would." Hungry, Long hoped they had food. He had to eat—and soon. If he needed to escape them too, he'd find a way. But for now, food was his priority.

They walked a few blocks to a run-down, four-apartment complex built after WWII, with tan walls and car ports held up by rusted poles. Reaching the one-bedroom unit upstairs, Tim pointed out, "This is it. You can sleep over in the corner on the bean bag chair, if ya want. How 'bout a peanut butter sandwich?"

"Yes, please." Excited to put something in his noisy stomach, Long devoured it. He then moved over to the bean bag chair and sat while Tim strummed his guitar and smoked more weed. Long now had time to think of what he'd say to his brother.

*I couldn't live at the Brown's house anymore. I hate it that you're alone, Duc, but I can't go back. You understand. She was mean and she hurt me. I know I don't know these people, but they helped me escape the police. Not that it was a great idea…but I was desperate.*

Even though they fed him, Long still didn't know if he could trust these people or what he would do next. His mind exhausted itself rehearsing the possibilities until, reluctantly, he fell asleep.

At about eleven the next morning, Tim and Ellie came out of their bedroom, immediately lighting up a joint. Long kept to himself on his chair. Throughout the day, the couple's friends came over, always smoking pot, while Tim played the guitar. Tim and Ellie didn't work, just kind of existed.

"Are you from Vietnam?" asked Tim.

"Yes."

"What was it like there? Were you there during the war?"

"Yes, but I don't remember very much. Just soldiers grabbing me and my brother, putting us on a truck, then flying here."

"That's so cool! What about your parents? Are they still there?"

"I didn't have any parents."

Tim, now embarrassed, turned slightly red. "I'm sorry, little dude…What was it like there?"

Long hesitated, but then deciding Tim was of little threat, Long answered honestly, "We lived in a village. The older ladies took care of us. When the North Vietnamese army came to our village, we ran. Eventually, we saw the American soldiers who were taking the kids away. We went with them. We lived at a place called Camp Pendleton for a while, then they brought us to foster families."

"That's an amazing story. You seem really smart. What do you want to do when you grow up?"

No one had ever asked him this. "I don't know," Long said blankly.

Tim looked at the boy for a minute without saying anything, then picked up his guitar and strummed while taking the last puff of his joint.

After a few days of the same aimless routine, Tim, noticing that Long had barely looked up from his bean bag, asked Long, "Do you want to go back to yer family?"

Long didn't like being there—with the smoke, guitars, and people constantly wandering in and out of the apartment. Tired of just existing with these do-nothing people, and knowing that Duc and the Browns must be looking for him, he nodded, "yes." He really missed Duc, felt bad leaving him. Tim's friend had a car and drove Long back to Simi Valley. He dropped Long off a couple of blocks from the Brown's house, not wanting to get involved.

Long was afraid of Mrs. Brown and what she would do when he returned, but he couldn't think of anything else to do. He needed to be with Duc and let him know he's ok.

Duke answered the door, a giant smile breaking across his face.

"Long! Where have you been? I was so worried about you, little brother." Duke grabbed Long and squeezed him harder than he had ever been squeezed. It felt good, and he didn't want Duc to let go.

Mrs. Brown stormed into the room, arms flailing around her red face. "Do you know what trouble you caused me?" she berated. "I'm in big trouble with the social worker because of you! Who do you think you are taking off like that?"

Long glared at her, silent. He hated being back there.

## On to Oxnard

Several more years were endured in Simi Valley with the Browns, but finally their servitude ended. Long had learned the skill of hiding his feelings. He kept his rage inside and did what he was told. It was all he could do. He realized that he could not be out on his own, yet. He had figured that living with the pot-smoking people who did nothing would get him nowhere. While life with the Browns was awful, it was structured.

Relieved more than ever to see Fred and his wagon, Long and Duke, now young teens, were taken to a family in Oxnard, California, where they had to sleep on the floor, evoking fond memories of their homeland. Although they had no beds, this family gave them a warm welcome. The Kreigers had a teenager named Jeremy. Long and Duke slept on the first floor, the real bedrooms all on the second.

After being there for a several weeks, Jeremy came downstairs and laid beside Long in the middle of the night. At first surprised, but comforted by this friendly gesture, Long quickly became distressed and confused when Jeremy stuck his hand down Long's pants. Long didn't understand. He only knew that the closeness to someone felt nice. He liked the intimacy and attention, and never said anything to anyone about Jeremy. He liked Jeremy and his family. They didn't treat him like a servant but more like a family member. The boys ate at the dinner table and were included in the conversation, like a real family. An orphan's life in the foster care system usually meant no warmth, no human touch. At this house, with the Kreigers, the boys were included in everything, and it felt good.

## CHAPTER 9

# NORTHERN CALIFORNIA

Long and Duke spent several months at the Kreiger house, then bounced around the Oxnard area: a few weeks at one family, a few weeks at the next, then another family for about a year—nothing remarkable, just more of the same.

Mid-term in junior high, they were moved from Southern California to Northern California, to North Highland, just above Sacramento, to a predominantly black community. The boys stayed with one of the few white families. They attended Don Julio Junior High, Long and Duke, again, the only Asian kids in the school.

Long's locker in the hallway was on the bottom row. Days after starting school at Don Julio, white and black kids began gathering around Long's locker between classes to yell *Slant*, *Gook*, *Chink*, and other small-minded descriptors. Every day without ceasing, the bullies taunted and pushed Long. While he encountered this at other schools, the kids were bigger and meaner at Don Julio.

After weeks of being pushed, bumped, and screamed at for being a "Slant," Long could no longer nod, smile, and be polite—he went after the bullies. The rage of months energized him: neck muscles taut, jaw clenched, fists tight and muscles flexed.

Long growled, "I have had enough of you! This has to stop!" He thrust his fist, made strong from years of weeding and other manual labor, into one of the boys' groins. Screaming, the other boys piled on to help their now wounded comrade. The fight did not last long. A teacher bolted out of the classroom—he had a lot of practice—grabbed the boys and dragged them to the principal's office. All them were put into a room awaiting the principal for his proclamation and punishment, their only judge and jury. The black and white bullies glared hatefully at Long. Long glared back, unafraid.

The principal, Eric Jeffers, a large, powerful-looking black man, came out of his office and in his strong voice, asked what happened. Long answered, "Every day, they push me, call me *Slant*... it never stops. I couldn't take it anymore. I lost my cool."

The principal asked the other boys, both black and white, if this was true. One of the white boys, with an offensive so-what attitude, said "Yeah, it's true." The principal grabbed the boy, slamming him against the wall with so much force the boy's head bounced off the white cinder-block.

Jeffers spoke over his shoulder, "Long, you can leave." As Long headed out of the office, he heard the principal yelling, "You little pricks will back off, or you will deal with me. And it won't be pretty."

The top culprit got a different locker. Long never again got bullied.

Fights were not new to Long. He had gotten into a fight at every school he ever attended, even elementary school. Names like *Chink, Chinaman*, and *Slant* always greeted him. Don Julio Junior High was the first time someone in authority had ever stood up for him. Long the Observer concluded that the black principal had suffered the same bullying himself and was not going let it happen on his watch. After the incident, whenever Long saw Mr. Jeffers, he got a wink and a "How ya doin'?"

Long heard from friends that no one had ever taken on the school bullies, so he became a bit of a hero at Don Julio for his bravery. Duc told him afterward, "I'm so proud of you taking on these assholes. They didn't see it comin'. Really cool." Duc's respect was worth everything to Long—respect from his only family.

## CHAPTER 10

# HIGH SCHOOL

The boys attended high school in Rio Linda, which Long called a low-income city with rednecks. Raised trucks, fitted with rifle racks behind the front seats and loaded with baseball bats instead of firearms, roamed the streets. Long witnessed a KKK march at the high school, white sheet wardrobe included. No violence ensued, but Long wondered, *why is there hate based on skin color? People are people.* Like the fighting years ago in Vietnam, it made no sense to Long.

america.

**Duke**

Duke was the life of the party in high school: good-looking, tall, and extremely popular. From the boys' delivery to the United States as children, through the foster family journey, Duc embraced becoming "Duke," becoming an American. Duke learned the language quickly, made lots of friends, wore trendy clothes, and grew his wavy black hair rock-star long, shaped to be messy-fashionable. Duke became a cool Asian-American. He watched out for Long but now only out of the corner of his eye, his focus now on being popular, chasing girls, and looking cool. Duke did odd jobs, saving most of the money he earned to buy an impressive 1967 Chevy Impala, metallic blue, lowered with spinner hubcaps. It had dual exhausts and made a menacing noise upon acceleration—the perfect party car.

One day while Duke was hanging out in the gym with a few cheerleaders, joking around and having fun, Long walked through, taking a shortcut between classes. Duke invited him over to join the party. Long reluctantly walked over and was introduced by Duke, "This is my little brother, Long."

"He's so cute!" proclaimed one of the cheerleaders.

Shy and embarrassed, Long forced a smile, gave a short waist-high wave, and left. Duke always warned Long never to follow his lead. The outgoing Duke drank, smoked pot, partied, and took risks—things he didn't want for his little brother. Unlike Long, Duke was popular; everyone knew him, and he was always in the middle of things.

Long rarely saw Duke. He played football, ran track, starred on the wrestling team. Duke fit in with every high school clique: he got along with the stoners, the brainiacs, the jocks. Long listened to his brother's advice and forged his own path.

"When the crowd zigs, I zag," became Long's mantra.

While Duke sought the spotlight, Long preferred the shadows. The brothers could not have been more different, yet they loved and watched over each other every day. Their bond was forever, from bridges, to bowls of rice, to running from the tanks, they could never be separated.

The day after the Long's shortcut across the basketball court, Long's teacher had a visitor, who entered the class and whispered something into her ear. The information had his teacher fighting back tears and looking toward Long, her face in shock. After the messenger left, she asked Long to come with her to the principal's office. There, he saw his then foster parents, the principal, and a school counselor, all looking uncomfortably somber. His foster mother with great difficulty in a choked voice said, "Duke is in the hospital. He was in a very bad car accident, Long."

Duke had been drag racing his Chevy Impala after cutting school when a car pulled out from an alley. Duke tried to turn to avoid the car emerging from the side street, but hit the car he was racing. The front wheels turned, caught the tire's edge at speed, and flipped the car. Duke's seatbelt wasn't on. He was thrown from the car and now in critical shape.

A fog gathered in Long's head. Terrified, for the first time in his life, he felt truly alone. He shook, unable to control himself. His foster parents drove Long to the hospital, where Duke lay with wires and lines attached to him everywhere. He was not awake. The doctor explained to Long, Duke's only real family, that his brother was "brain-dead" from the accident, and that he would not wake up.

Long looked at his brother, sleeping in a maze of wires and gadgetry, and could not comprehend. *Duc is breathing.* Long protested in the small hospital room, "He has to be ok. I cannot lose him! He is my brother!" Long cried, for the second time in his life.

The doctor explained to Long that although parts of his brother's body worked, his brain did not, and he would never wake up. "He cannot live without help from machines," the doctor informed Long somberly.

Long, with the help of his foster parents, had to make the decision to let Duc go.

*Now I know there is no God*, Long concluded. He always saw his brother as better, thought he had more to contribute to society. *Why was he taken? There's something wrong with that.*

"Why take a great seed and leave a not-so-great seed to live?" Long agonized, speaking his thoughts into his empty room. Long felt alone, now he had no one.

Falling deep into a depression, Long went through the motions of life, but with a bottomless emptiness inside. Though he ate, slept, studied, and went to school, a dark mood constantly enveloped him. Lost. Downhearted. Day and night, even in his sleep, he felt sadness to the point of pain, the longing for his brother worse than any hunger he had ever experienced. Long operated on autopilot. He sat in the back row in class, allowed his hair to grow long. He felt alone, isolated with no sense of the future and no sense of hope. He just existed.

Alone in America.

## CHAPTER 11

# THE GIFT OF BEING A JANITOR

During Long's year of fog, he had a lot of time to think. What happened to him? Why did he live here, what purpose in life did he have? Did he have a future? Over the months, he came to realize that his life as he knew it at age fifteen, remained a life of dependency. He was dependent for everything—for food, for shelter, for clothing. Some of his foster families had good intentions but showed no connection to him beyond fulfilling his basic needs as they were contracted. The fog brought to him a revelation. He had to be able to take care of himself, answer to no one, become *independent.*

His year-long depression made one thing clear. To be truly independent, he had to earn his own money.

Long made a plan setting an ambitious goal for himself—save $5,000 by the time he turned sixteen. After wondering briefly how he would do that he began looking for jobs, through posted "help wanted" signs, ads in newspapers, and the school bulletin board. His best lead was a hand-written 3 x 5 card tacked onto the main school bulletin board: "Wanted. Janitor to work night shift. 916-234-5876." *I have that kind of experience, cleaning and picking up at all my foster homes. This will be easy.* He went to a pay phone, called the number, and arranged to meet Steve, the man who posted the job.

Long got the night janitorial job working every evening from five to eleven p.m. or later, cleaning office buildings. For Long, the job was a gift, his greatest good fortune. He worked the way he did for his foster families, but now he earned money, receiving cash for the hours he worked. In those same office buildings, Long discovered a treasure chest of information that helped him meet his first financial goal. *The Wall Street Journal, Barron's, Fortune* magazine, and other investment publications he found in trash bins, offered an enormous amount of useful information that he studied with great care. Each night, he collected whatever business magazines he found tossed in the trash and brought them home to study, reading again and again—in time using them as the basis of his own eventual investment philosophy.

Life now changed for Long. He'd found an interest; he'd formed a solid plan to become independent financially.

After school, he biked to the head janitor's house, and Steve gave him a ride in his truck to the office buildings. His boss Steve always considered Long reliable: the kid never missed a day, never slacked off or called in sick. Other kids he'd hired in the past had gotten bored with the work, or were just plain lazy, with plenty of excuses to call-off work. But Long was a real find. He did the best job cleaning and got more work done than two of his counterparts. Steve appreciated Long's work ethic and reliability, and in time, made him a supervisor. Long managed and trained the other cleaners and became a valuable partner to Steve. While Long started at four dollars an hour, after becoming supervisor, he'd doubled his salary to eight dollars an hour in just a few months.

America!

Steve paid him cash, in an envelope, but Long never counted it. His relationship with Steve became one based on trust. Long attached a plastic bag to his janitor's cart and gathered journals and magazines which he saved for future reading and study. Steve introduced Long to *Money* magazine, which helped Long understand some of the terms in the more difficult technical publications.

With an eye toward investing, Long started following companies too, initially concentrating on airlines. While he eventually learned technical finance terms in addition to analyzing stock prices, he began looking at the *leadership* of the companies. Long the Observer came to understand that *people* run companies. This simple revelation became one of Long's core principles of investing. For example, after learning about Frank Lorenzo, the CEO of Texas Air, he was able to make a connection to some "funny business" at the top when Texas Air eventually went out of business.

He consumed information voraciously about company leadership, looking not only at official, public statements such as stock reports, but also at speeches, the CEO's lifestyle, anything he could get his hands on. He went to the library to study great financial success stories such as Andrew Carnegie, JP Morgan, Jay Gould, and Cornelius Vanderbilt. He found his Opportunity and his Gift through access to all of this information collected being a janitor.

Long saved every dollar he made. He never spent his money on things he'd like to have. So, before the age of sixteen, he'd met his goal of earning and saving $5,000. At the bank down the street from school, he converted cash to a cashier's check for $5,000, cut school, got on a bus, and traveled to the Charles Schwab office. He approached the clerk and told her that he wanted to open an account. She asked for identification, and after reviewing it, told him that he was not old enough to open an account, and that he would need his parents' co-signature. This barrier did not stop Long. He waited until the clerk left for a break, then approached the new clerk with his request, now "signed" by his foster parents.

Long now owned a Charles Schwab account worth $5,000.

AMERICA!

At first, Long invested in airline stocks, then beef processing stocks. Fees for transactions at the time cost $150-$200 per trade, so Long needed to be judicious. Also, they charged another fee for odd-lot trades, so Long made sure to buy enough so he would hit even lots of one hundred, two hundred, or three hundred shares in order to save money on buying and selling.

He studied, traded with clear-eyed caution, and never lost money on any of his investments.

Any penny Long made, he invested. He collected bottles to trade in for cash that he invested. After little league games, he collected empty cans and bottles on the bleachers and ground, then dumpster-dived for more bottles to cash in. Everything he collected, he converted to cash to put into his Schwab account.

*For a kid, I have a lot of money.*

He asked himself, "If I make fifty dollars after commissions on an investment, how many bottles would I have to collect to make that much money? How many hours of janitorial work would it take to make fifty bucks?"

As a minor, he lived with his foster family, had food and shelter, and received clothes from the social workers, so everything he made as a janitor or collecting bottles, he invested. He didn't buy candy bars like other kids because he saw those dollars as investment dollars.

# CHAPTER 12

## THE ARMY OPPORTUNITY

Now a junior at Rio Linda High, Long met a recruiter from the Army National Guard who visited the campus to make a presentation to the students. The recruiter told the boys that if they joined the Army National Guard they could stay in high school and do their Army training during the summer. The first summer after their junior year, they'd attend boot camp, and the second summer after their senior year, they'd get AIT (Advanced Infantry Training).

Long figured, *how perfect! I can earn more money in the military to save and invest.* He signed up right then. The first summer, at Fort Sill, Oklahoma for artillery training, Long volunteered for Forward Observer training. As a forward observer, often called the most dangerous position in the entire Army, Long would earn extra pay.

Long the Observer was now a forward observer who crawled ahead of the main troop positions to locate the enemy and call in artillery strikes. Forward observers give the coordinates of the enemy positions, and if accurate, the artillery strikes demoralize or kill the enemy. If inaccurate, forward observers can be hit by friendly fire, their own army's artillery strikes. The position is more dangerous than others, as the enemy routinely seeks out forward observers to neutralize them. But because the position offered higher pay, Long volunteered. *All the more to invest*, he thought.

The Army provided all food and shelter, so Long saved a lot of money. Every payday, Long stood in line to get paid. He received his check, then stood in another line to get it cashed, then went to the post exchange to have the cash converted to a cashier's check. He collected these cashier's checks in his locker, hidden under folded clothes, all saved so he could invest them later.

The Army provided other money-making opportunities for Long as well. At night, most soldiers went into town to drink, watch girls in topless bars, and spend their money on booze and fun—unless they had the dreaded, unavoidable guard duty, a responsibility rotated among the soldiers.

Long saw another way to earn cash. Each day, Long checked the guard duty roster, and approached whoever was slated that night, "I see that you have guard duty tonight…"

"Yeah, I hate it. All night carrying that damn rifle on my shoulder."

Long quickly offered, "I would be happy to do it for you if you like. I need some extra money if you don't mind."

"You bet! How much?"

"I'll do it for $5 if that's ok."

"That's a deal. Thanks, my friend. I owe you."

This enterprise proved very successful as most soldiers dreaded walking the perimeter of the base in the middle of the night, in uniform and carrying a rifle which seemed only to get progressively heavier as the shift wore on. Long routinely took over this duty for them, and of course saved all of this extra money.

A second enterprise Long discovered was doing laundry for his fellow soldiers. He told them to leave their laundry bag with him, he'd launder their clothes and put them back in the bag, clean and folded. He had six or seven loads going every night. More cash. More savings. More investment.

Long's third enterprise, KP (Kitchen Patrol), was another responsibility most soldiers would do anything to avoid. The assigned soldier had to get up at four in the morning, report to the kitchen, work the entire day serving, cleaning tables, doing dishes, then serving again, and cleaning again. All rosters were assigned in pencil, so Long studied the roster, found the soldier assigned to KP, made the offer to take his spot, and penciled in his own name—for cash. This service also became very popular with Long's soldier-mates. More savings. More investment.

The military insists on routine inspections in the barracks, a form of Army discipline, a show of readiness. Boots must be spit-shined and perfect; belt buckles needed to be shined bright with brass polish. Beds had to be made tight with hospital corners, so that when a Sergeant inspector dropped a quarter on the bed, it had to bounce. If the coin didn't bounce, the soldier failed, his furloughs canceled. Inspections created another money-making opportunity for Long.

On Inspection Day, Long made sure that he scheduled himself for KP. If on KP, he'd not take part in the inspection. Before the day of inspection, Long offered boot shining, buckle polishing, and bed-making services to his comrades. He worked fast, very good at those jobs. It became an irreplaceable service for his lazier fellow soldiers. For Long, it meant more money earned and saved.

By the end of the first summer, he amassed a nice pile of cashier's checks, all to be invested.

The second summer brought even more opportunities. At AIT, Advanced Infantry Training, Long served as a cannon crewman. He re-introduced the same money-making services he offered the first summer, but now much better, because Long perfected each service. At AIT, the soldiers had more time off than the basic training in the first summer. They had more weekends off, so Long adjusted his pricing model for weekend guard duty services. He charged based on how desperate his customers presented themselves, with pricing ranging from one dollar up to five. For his laundry service, he realized he didn't need to buy soap, threw his own clothes in with one of his customer's, who'd already purchased soap, therefore saving on his own laundry expenses.

Long developed a new product he offered the second summer—pay phone services. Fellow soldiers lined up at the pay phones, especially before the weekends, to talk to their girlfriends or to find a party. Long went to the bank and bought bags of quarters, posting himself in the pay phone area. Long filled his multi-pocketed infantry pants with inventory from his bags of quarters. When soldiers ran out of quarters for the pay phone, Long was right there with his valuable service—three quarters for a dollar. This became a popular and profitable service. More cash. More to invest.

## CHAPTER 13

# COLLEGE AND
# SERIOUS INVESTING

Long did not do well in high school. His lukewarm interest in school went cold after his brother's death. His objective was only to sit in back of class, do the minimum, and blend in. Long's real focus in high school was to earn cash on summer Army duty and nighttime janitorial work and learn as much as possible about finance. That drove him, not high school subjects. Long wanted to amass wealth, gain independence, and rely on no one.

He heard community college will take you if you have a heartbeat, so Long enrolled. He knew he'd have to make up for his bad grades in high school and improve his academic record. He chose business for his major and continued to study his passion; he learned from the greats: Andrew Carnegie, JP Morgan, Jay Gould, and Cornelius Vanderbilt. *How did they amass fortunes? How did they think? What drove them?*

After community college, Long enrolled at Sacramento State University, and graduated successfully with a Bachelor of Science degree in Finance.

While in college, Long made only one friend, a Vietnamese boy named Billy who was in school merely to impress his parents, not because he wanted to study. At first, Long didn't think much of Billy, especially because he was a flashy dresser. Long didn't focus on making friends, his goal, always, to amass wealth and earn independence.

In one of his early classes while taking a test, one with a Scantron answer sheet where bubbles next to the answer are filled in with pencil, Long noticed Billy struggling, not completing the test questions. Without really knowing why, Long slid his paper over to the side of the desk so that Billy could copy his answers. Billy did and, later, remarkably got an A in the class.

After that unexpected assistance, Billy found Long walking along the quad, "Hey, where ya goin'?"

"I'm going to the student union to study."

"Let's go eat," Billy suggested to a reticent Long, who nevertheless followed him to the cafeteria. When Billy whipped out a $100 bill to pay for their lunch, Long showed no change of expression, just a slight nod of the head.

Days after that initial lunch, Billy found Long, who had begrudgingly told him of his favorite place on campus. Sure enough, Long was nearly always at his usual spot in the library, an old dark section in the back with run-down carpets, Long's preferred place to study. He enjoyed the quiet, the solitude, the privacy of having his own place to study for his classes, and of course to be nearer to the writings of his famous mentors. Most students went to the new, shiny, bright section of the library. Billy frequently found Long in his quiet place, invited him to dinner, and always had cash—$100 bills—and always paid. Billy doggedly invited Long to go out for the weekend, but Long had always refused. He had to study.

One weekend, Long relented and agreed to go with him. Long met him at the college, where Billy drove up in his gold BMW M3 sedan. Billy didn't drive the car; he had someone else in the driver's seat. Long and Billy sat in the back. Behind them, five other BMWs followed. *These friends are a motley crew*, Long thought. *Asian gangs?* Unlike his shady companions, shod in tattoos, leather jackets, and expensive ripped jeans, Long dressed for business in slacks and a nice shirt, always ironed. *Dress like the businessman I will be some day.* The gang liked and looked up to Billy, always the center of attention, The Leader.

Unlike traditional domestic gangs like the Bloods, Crips, and Surenos, Vietnamese gangs did not claim territories. They drove around in expensive cars.

"Where are we going?" Long asked, but soon realized they were just cruising around town. *This is a huge waste of time – I could be studying*, thought Long. They went to one of the gang member's houses with no parents present, a nice two-story Normandy-style home, which surprised Long considering who lived there. Everyone wanted to sit or stand next to Billy because of his magnetic personality. All the members wanted to ride with him, but Billy chose Long to ride along. Their money-making scheme centered on betting, and Long found out that Billy acted as a bookie for students, making money on every basketball and football game, working the point spread and taking a commission.

After about a year of friendship, Billy asked Long if he wanted to meet his family. Long said yes, and they drove to Billy's parents' house in San Jose. When they pulled up, Long was surprised to see the house looked modest, a single story 50's tract house with a couple of bedrooms and one bath. Long soon determined these humble Vietnamese immigrants had no idea what Billy did but felt proud that he had earned enough money to drive a BMW and help them financially when they needed help.

Billy's mom rushed to feed Long and take care of him. How many years had it been since Long felt this kind of warmth from people who didn't need payment to tend to his needs? Billy's parents, such a kind, loving family, welcomed him unconditionally. Oddly, over the course of their friendship, Long never saw where Billy himself lived. Billy had always found Long in the library, grabbed his books, dropped them in a bag, and said "Let's go!"

Meeting Billy's family made Long feel closer to his friend. He could almost imagine that Billy was a normal, enterprising young man. But several months after their trip to San Jose, things took a turn. Billy called at midnight, tension in his voice, "Long, you gotta help me out!"

Long heard desperation in Billy's voice, not the usual calm and cool leader. "I need your help to pick up a dead body in the Bay Area before dawn."

Shocked, Long said "No, I can't do that…I need to work."

Billy did more than run a friendly gambling operation on campus, taking sports bets from students. He also made loans, not to students, but to others—loans with high interest and high risk. These loans, if not paid, would be met with "reminders," followed by increasing punishment for not making payments. Billy's band of followers executed his plan, as Billy rarely got involved in day-to-day operations anymore.

One of Billy's customers had been stiffing him, not paying anything. His customer, Bobby Tran, had family problems, a sick wife, and three children to feed. He pleaded to Billy's people to give him more time, "I have to buy food! I have to pay hospital bills. I'll pay you a little, but I can't get it all right now!"

Billy's orders were clear: business is business; punishment must be meted out with increasing harshness. Billy never took it all the way. His customers usually found a way to pay him back. But Billy ran a business, and business has rules. However, Billy's team went too far this time, and Bobby Tran was dead under a bridge, brought there after the severe punishment turned fatal. Billy froze when his guy told him. He didn't know what to do. Anger turned to panic; he never had to deal with a body before. *Long is smart. He'll figure it out*, Billy told himself.

But after Long hung up the phone that night, he never spoke to Billy again. He never learned the circumstances surrounding the dead body, who helped Billy, how the body got there, or what Billy had to do with it. Long never even knew Billy's last name, and often wondered what had happened to him.

**Graduation**

On the day of graduation from Sacramento State, after all the robed graduating students left with their proud parents, family, and friends to go celebrate, Long walked to the courtyard outside the graduation ceremonies. He stood alone, chest puffed out a bit. He felt proud of his degree and reflected on what he had accomplished so far—a degree, a good-size portfolio, and cash.

Long had no family to say how proud they felt, but he never had a family. Except Duc.

What he was really proud of was how much he had amassed by graduation at age 21:

$57,000 in his portfolio, plus "some cash."

He did it by spending no money unless absolutely necessary. *Invest everything.* He kept his accomplishment secret. No one knew that he did this by never eating out, never spending, not even on French fries. He bummed rides rather than paying for the bus or taxis, and only spent on absolute necessities—rent, tuition, books, and one small meal a day purchased from the day-old section at the back of the grocery store.

Unlike most savers, Long realized that every dollar he did *not* spend could be *invested.* Money earned more money. One thousand dollars today will be two thousand dollars in seven years, four thousand in fourteen, eight thousand in twenty-one years. He did not learn this in class. He learned it by absorbing and internalizing all the valuable information he had collected while cleaning office buildings and by studying the great millionaires at his cherished place, the library.

## CHAPTER 14

# DEAN WITTER

After graduation, Long continued his drive to nurture his financial bottom line. Accumulation equals independence. He wanted access to a place that could feed his insatiable need for information on companies and investing. His roommate and friend, Gerald, worked as an intern at Dean Witter, an unpaid position assisting brokers by gathering information. Knowing Long's passion for investing, having watched him run to pay phones between classes to get stock quotes and listening to him talk ceaselessly with great enthusiasm about companies, Gerald introduced him to the broker he was interning for.

Gerald worked for Marv Larkin, a young broker who recommended and sold stocks to his clients based on "juice sheets." Juice sheets listed stocks promoted by Dean Witter because they had underwritten the stock or had some other kind of interest and earned extra commission for the brokers. Marv spent his day pushing these stocks, making him somewhat of an office hotshot. But Long considered those tactics shady and unscrupulous.

Though Long didn't agree with pushing stocks based solely on the commission you'd make, it didn't stop him from getting hired by Marv Larkin as an intern. Naturally, Long did well there. So well, in fact, Marv started ignoring Gerald, and eventually Gerald just did not show up for work. Long felt terrible about affecting Gerald's job. *I wasn't trying outshine him. I'm just so consumed with stocks, I didn't think about him. I need to do better and not be so selfish. I must work on this!*

Long considered working at Dean Witter another Gift and Opportunity, a lot like his job as a janitor. Even though he didn't get paid as an intern, Long had access to infinite information about companies. He read recommendations generated from home office on the green on black CRT (cathode ray tube) computer screens and also devoured piles of brochures covering companies, neatly stacked on shelves in the office. He stayed at the office well into the night.

After months working with Long, Marv said, "Long, you're here at all hours, so here's a key to the office. Don't tell anyone cuz it's against the rules, OK?"

Long gained people's trust through his honest approach, incomparable work ethic, and great analysis.

David Nakamoto, the largest producer in the office, built a sizeable business and clientele in the Sacramento Dean Witter office. He specialized in serving Japanese customers: doctors, lawyers, and other wealthy Japanese who depended on Nakamoto to make investment decisions for them. He had binders of clients and did his own research in addition to looking at the juice sheets. His work for his clients became an early form of a mutual fund, with Nakamoto as the fund manager. Nakamoto hired interns to help him with his independent research. Marv suggested to David Nakamoto that he meet Long. They had a short and cordial initial meeting.

Mr. Nakamoto took notice of Long, always there late in the evenings, sitting at the green terminal. He saw Long there every Saturday with the loaf of bread he brought and ate throughout the long day of researching, scouting, and observing how companies ran—and most importantly—the people that ran them.

Months after their initial meeting, Mr. Nakamoto invited Long to lunch. Long was impressed with Nakamoto, and Nakamoto with Long. After that lunch, they spent many hours discussing companies. Long shared his extensive knowledge and research with David Nakamoto. Eventually, Nakamoto offered Long a job working exclusively for him. He paid Long out of his own pocket for analysis and recommendations.

Nakamoto set up a desk in his office where Long could work and where the two men could collaborate throughout the day. Over time, Nakamoto included some of Long's stock picks in his recommendations to clients, and eventually Long made most of the stock picks that Mr. Nakamoto recommended.

Long, now fondly called "Longer" by David, recommended Nike, then a relatively new company, which turned out to be an extraordinary stock pick.

"The owners of Nike don't think about a product as a product; they analyze the market," Long said to Nakamoto. "They've re-invented the shoe business based on *end use*: track, cross-country running, basketball, and other niches like "everyday casual" they coined. Nike *created markets* that didn't exist before. As an example, they invented the waffle pattern for running shoes to gain traction. One morning, Bill Bowerman, the founder and CEO, helped make breakfast with his wife. Making waffles that morning, he focused on the waffle iron they used, and Bill Bowerman came up with the idea to try the pattern on track shoes. The idea worked, and Bowerman patented the Nike Waffle Trainer!"

Mr. Nakamoto grinned like a proud parent as Long made his case. The Long-Nakamoto investment happened based on how the founders thought and created, not only on their financials.

Nakamoto's clients did well, far exceeding the performance of the office and market in total, all with the help of Long's research and recommendations. After several years of working with David Nakamoto, Long knew more than his boss, exceeding him in technical analysis and intuition, but Nakamoto had the relationships, connections, and personality to drive the business. "Longer" took the role of the engine behind the recommendations.

Mr. Nakamoto gave Long a goal of increasing his clients' portfolio values by twenty percent a year. Long thought twenty percent was too low and too easy with all the information available to him. They exceeded the twenty percent goal with an impressive thirty-percent increase. Nakamoto paid Long $40,000 per year out of his own pocket, very good pay for the time.

Nakamoto's clients had complete faith in him, and in turn, he had complete faith in Long. Clients trusted Mr. Nakamoto with $250,000 each and asked him to invest that sum as he saw fit. With his research and collaboration with Long, they exceeded $50,000 of growth in a year for each of the $250,000 investments. Mr. Nakamoto was a hero to his clients, and with his success, he bought a house in the Sacramento area for $750,000 cash.

Nakamoto, in his forties, married a lawyer who worked for Adventist Health System. After working for Mr. Nakamoto for three years and hearing about the significant changes in his wife's business, Long began deeply researching healthcare as an industry. He specifically looked at HMO's, Health Maintenance Organizations. These medical organizations were pioneers, and ultimately changed the delivery paradigm of how health care works in the United States.

HMO's, unlike traditional insurance plans, paid the participating doctors *in advance* of delivering service to their patients. HMO's paid the doctors a fixed rate based on the number of patients they had in the plan. The doctors would be paid whether they saw patients or not. The payment method was called "capitation," or "per head." HMO's philosophy: maintain patients' health to prevent illnesses where possible—HMO's paid doctors to keep patients well, not just when they were sick or injured. The healthier the patient population, the more money the doctors could make. In theory, a doctor with a completely healthy group of patients would get paid and never see a patient. On the other hand, if doctors had a very sick patient population, they would make less money than the traditional "fee for service" model. HMO's had the paradigm-busting incentive—keep patients well.

Long studied these plans religiously. He learned that HMO companies, like Kaiser Permanente and Family Health Plan, paid staff doctors a salary, called staff model plans. Long learned of other types of HMOs too such as the "IPA," Independent Practice Association model, where private doctors with their own practices would contract with the HMO and get paid a per-patient fee (capitation) for seeing the HMO's patients.

Long concluded through research that these kinds of plans would change the course of health care delivery. He believed that the traditional insurance model, where a patient pays twenty percent of the cost and the insurance company pays eighty percent, sounded unsustainable. There was no incentive for insurance companies to control healthcare costs. If healthcare costs went up, it would raise insurance rates paid by employers for their employees. Soon, healthcare costs for employers became the second largest expense after salary expense. The solution for employers? —offer less insurance, or no insurance, or make the employee pay a larger portion of the premium. To Long, there were only bad options until HMOs came on the scene, offering complete healthcare at significantly reduced premiums for employers.

Long studied the early entrant HMO companies, examined their financial model, their operations, and as always, their leadership. He compared one company to another and made recommendations to Mr. Nakamoto for his clients. This strategy proved an enormous success, getting Mr. Nakamoto's clients invested early in a monumental sea change in the U.S. health insurance industry.

## CHAPTER 15

# TURNING POINT

Investment businesses always need the *new idea* to offer clients something different, something with high potential returns, to demonstrate the investment company's value. Over time, Long realized that so many factors affect the market that there would never be a winning strategy *in the short term* that constantly feeds the need to show success. Investors react to headlines with fear and are cautious about putting their trust in investment advisors who desire to be right most of the time. Most investors share the desire to outsmart the market, sell when high, get out when the market falls, and get back in when the market turns positive.

But Long realized no human being is that good. *Even I am not that good. I need to change my life, financially. I'm going to invest based on my own research and take a long-term approach.* He knew that this long-term approach would not work in the investment advisory business. It doesn't meet the need to find something new, to stay ahead of the inexplicable changes in the market, and play the role of servant to the widely ranging human emotions that understandably come with investing and gambling one's future.

Long decided he would become his own investment advisor for his own portfolio, think long-term, and only invest in *companies that would outlive him.* This became Long's guiding principle.

*Companies that will outlive me.* Go Long.

Long developed this enlightened approach over many years of success in his own investing. Invest everything, spend only when necessary. Always pay for the stocks you buy and don't buy on margin. That way you get joy when the market is up, and you get joy when the market is down. Long explained to those who asked, "When the market's down, that's a gift and an opportunity to buy more at a cheaper price. I am happy in either direction as long as I have strong companies in my portfolio that will outlive me."

He decided that he wanted a job with a salary that would provide the basic necessities of life, but also provide him insight into how companies operate from the inside. Understanding this would make him an even better investor, learning how companies work when you are part of one.

Long decided all he needed was a job that provided $1,000 per month. *I will eat very little, drink only water, and rent an apartment with maybe one roommate. I'll build my portfolio every year, put all extra money into it, so that by the time I'm old, I'll be very wealthy.*

When Long told David Nakamoto of his decision to leave, Nakamoto didn't try to dissuade him.

"It's hard to try to figure out the market short-term—there's so much emotion," said Long. "You know, I like companies where I respect the management, the product, its recurring revenue. They fluctuate with the market but will be there for a long time and have continued growth because of their business model. That's good for my portfolio, but not good for the buy and sell world that investment advisors need to be successful. This just isn't for me anymore. I want to work inside a company to find out how they work, how decisions are made, how management operates and treats their customers and employees."

"I really get it, Longer," David said affectionately. "You need to move in another direction, and I respect that. I will really miss you. You're the best analyst I've ever worked with. You're a whole lot better than the guys at the corporate office, between you and me."

They hugged, something Long never did. He felt sad, but the logic of his decision drove him.

"Longer" and David kept in contact and remain friends today.

# CHAPTER 16

## A REAL JOB

Long scoured the ads for a job in finance, preferably in the health care industry, eager to get into the real world where people work hard to get a paycheck, pay their rent, and put food on the table. He wanted to see how management operated, how companies made decisions, and what drove those decisions.

Long dressed for business success, even when working for no pay as an intern. *You must be professional in appearance, hair short, shirt tucked in, pants pressed, shoes shined.* He did not see this as superficial but rather as a badge that says, "I'm here to work, and I will give my full attention to the task in accomplishing what you want me to."

He interviewed with Fortune 500 companies. These large conglomerates mostly looked at the quality of credentials more than the person. He discovered that his degree from Sacramento State impressed no one.

These companies looked for people with Yale, Harvard, Wharton School of Business pedigrees. Long's

Sacramento State degree, combined with his small Asian stature, led to no job offers. Long was disappointed to find the companies looked more at the trappings and appearances than at *the person*—not at the worth I bring, how hard I've worked, what I've accomplished, and how I think.

Long changed his focus and came across a regional healthcare system called Golden Valley Health Center. Founded in 1972 as a hospital-operated, not-for-profit migrant health center, the operation opened its first medical and dental clinic in 1974, called Merced Family Health Centers, later changed to Golden Valley Health Center.

Their mission? "To improve the health of our patients by providing quality, primary health care services to people in the communities we serve regardless of language, financial, or cultural barriers." This felt right to Long, himself an immigrant. He knew he'd feel at home with people of very different, but familiar, circumstances. He landed a job in accounting where he moved up the ladder fast, to controller.

Long grasped how things operated right away, honed his observation skills, absorbed both the operation and the company culture. He learned how the operation was funded, how spending decisions were made, how personnel decisions happened, and how a not-for-profit is really a *for-profit*. Even a not-for-profit has to bring in more revenue than expenses to survive.

Long worked for the chief financial officer, Guy Ramirez, a stocky, likeable gentleman with a broad smile and a caring persona.

"How you doing, Long?" Guy would say when they passed. Guy frequently solicited Long's opinions on projects he was working on. Long had excellent ideas, but never volunteered information. His deference to senior management caused Long to speak only when spoken to and made him reticent to offer his viewpoints before being asked.

All senior management at this operation had a sense of a broader mission, beyond just earning a paycheck, scoring a raise, or being promoted. They had a mission to take care of those most in need, those who do some of the hardest work in the American workforce. Agriculture, the predominant occupation in the area, called for back-breaking hunched picking of crops, was most in demand. These laborers did the jobs that immigrants of several generations prior abandoned for more prestigious positions in manufacturing or service industries. Migrant workers often had severe back problems, sores, soft tissue injuries, as well as infections from working with fertilizers and pesticides. They worked for minimum wage at best, and for less with the more unscrupulous employers.

Families often lived in small one-or-two-bedroom houses with eight or nine people under one roof, three generations living in one house, common. Providing food came first. Healthcare? Being hurt or sick was mostly ignored in favor of earning that next day of pay.

Like the rest of management, Guy had a passion for their mission, to take care of their patients while giving them complete respect. He understood their drive to be faithful to their jobs so they could provide for their families, their pride profound. Manhood meant bringing home a paycheck.

Long was quick to adopt this mission and to feel the compassion exhibited by the employees at Golden Valley Health Center. As a junior executive in the finance department, Long learned that decisions were often made based on a patient's need, and not the financial impact of certain actions. Long appreciated this and saw his personal mission as "watching the organization's pennies so that the dollars could be spent for the health of their patient population." Long had a lot of practice watching pennies, ever since his first day stepping on American soil.

# CHAPTER 17

---

# DATING?

L ong had never taken a girl on a date, had only a few friends and none extremely close. Part of Long's journey included disappointment with relationships, brought on by his many foster "so-called" families that never allowed closeness, never allowed trust or affection. Long interacted with people, helped them often, made money from them, but never allowed anyone to get close. Cautious with all relationships, he did not allow himself closeness for fear of disappointment.

While Long rarely socialized, his work at Golden Valley Health Center offered a way to meet people. The center had created a number of outreach programs to let the community know they were there, to offer screenings to catch diseases or injuries that people might not know they have or have been ignoring. Many of the outreach programs happened in the evening.

Guy, passing by Long on his way to his office, said "Hey Long, we do these outreach programs you've heard about to let the community know about us. You've seen the entries in the books for the costs. Wanna come with me to volunteer tonight?"

"Yes, of course I'd love to."

Long wanted to do this, wanted to help others, also wanted to add to his observation arsenal about how companies ran.

Loan, a dentist at Golden Valley Health Center, volunteered that evening. Long spotted her immediately as they piled into one of the corporate vans going to the event. She immediately made an impression on him. *This girl is so beautiful, looks Vietnamese, I need to get the courage to talk with her*. Long felt something he'd never experienced—desire for someone else, for human interaction that isn't transactional. Once in the van, he looked over at her again, and she looked quickly at him, but then glanced away.

They both felt something. Long had never taken a girl on a date. Loan was almost as new to this as Long. She'd been out with another Vietnamese boy, Duong, a few times. Duong came from Vietnamese royalty. The family looted the country at the end of the war and headed to the US to spend it. Duong had been in the United States longer and knew his way around. Loan liked Duong, funny, well-off, and good-looking, but his family looked down on her father, a poor recent immigrant.

Long and Loan were assigned intake duties at his first volunteer event, getting people's names and demographic information to create a chart before their first screening. Impressed with Long's energy and ability to organize the tasks, his gentle demeanor and humility, Loan felt drawn to his quiet strength.

"Let's set up here. I've put together a sign-in sheet, including name, address, phone number, and insurance information," said Long.

"These people don't have insurance, I'm afraid," Loan said, smiling.

"I'm in Finance. I have to watch the pennies for the company. If they have insurance, it will help the company, so I need to ask anyway."

For Loan, Long appeared genuine, not from royalty and not manufactured. Long always spoke the truth, with a dry sense of humor.

Long felt himself drawn to Loan, her smile, her grace, her beauty. He watched people she interacted with at the volunteer event warm to her. Long experienced an energy, warmth, and closeness he'd not experienced since a little boy with Ba Phuong in Vietnam.

When Long learned that Loan sometimes went out with Duong, he realized he had competition and had to act fast. Adrenalin coursed through him. He knew that Loan, for him, was *the one*. He asked Loan to dinner and spent money like he'd never spent before. They had a great time, like they'd known each other forever: laughing, gossiping about work, then tearfully talking about their adventures getting to America. Long had so much fun with Loan, but felt a twinge when he had to part with money that he could have invested. No matter, he had to beat Duong.

# CHAPTER 18

## LOAN

In Vietnam, Loan's mother walked far from their village to find a new location for water for her family. Peppered with land mines, she triggered one, dying in the explosion.

After his wife's death, Tuan, Loan's father, became driven to create a better life for his family. He vowed to leave his war-torn homeland. A farmer, he had no savings and could provide only the basics to his children, sometimes not even that.

Loan grew up this way—and like Long—had a brother named Duc. The siblings knew nothing else, but felt safe and protected by their papa. Tuan scraped and saved for years after his wife's death and finally saved enough to buy gold nuggets, the ticket for a fishing boat to take him, his son and daughter to the first step in the journey to America, Malaysia. People who bought a passage on a fishing boat had to pack themselves into the bottom of the boat, shoulder to shoulder, barely able to find seating.

The more that the boatmen could stuff in, the higher the profits.

On the day of departure, Tuan, Loan and her brother Duc, hastened to the dock after spending several days gathering belongings worth taking: for Tuan, a second pair of pants, a second shirt, food and water, and the shoes that he wore; for Loan and Duc, each wore what they owned, and packed another shirt each. Loan took her favorite straw doll, Lan, which meant flower. At twelve, she felt too old for dolls, and yet she couldn't leave her childhood companion behind. The straw doll had comforted her at night when her mother didn't return home and during those anxious times when soldiers preyed on the weak in her village.

Loan's family climbed aboard, directed by the smelly, ruddy, unkempt captain down narrow stairs with metal handrails into what used to be a cargo hold for the daily catch. The putrid fish smell so strong, Loan tried not to disgrace herself and her father by throwing up her meager breakfast.

Her father whispered, "All will be better in the new land. Think of what life will be like in America. Lots of food, new clothes, a nice place to live, and peace. No soldiers, no guns, no land mines."

Loan felt better.

They heard the ropes tossed back to the dock and the motor's roar before the boat began to move, the first leg of the journey taking them closer to America. Despite the crowding and pushing, Tuan put his arms around his daughter and son, and they slept.

The family spent days at sea sitting in the cargo hold, accustomed to the calm rolling, droning of motors, and chit chat from the other sardined passengers. Once in a while, people laughed at jokes, but for the most part, they sat on the floor, lost in their own thoughts, dreaming of what their lives will be like in America.

After three days, the seas developed into a violent thrashing. Tuan felt the boat attempt a steep climb, then drop, the lurching so violent, the passengers screamed, vomited, and sobbed in fear. Water first leaked in, then poured in to fill the cargo area where everyone sat huddled. Fearful, then panicked, passengers got up, pushed for a spot on the stairs to find the deck and air. Tuan grabbed Loan and Duc, squeezing the three of them up the packed stairwell to the deck. Once topside, they felt the boat rise skyward on a mountain of water, then twist to the side, tossing its passengers into the cold sea. Tuan could swim; his children could not. He held on to Loan and Duc with the strongest grip he could summon.

Now capsized, the boat's propeller turned in the wind. Tuan floated on his back, Loan in one arm, Duc in the other, treading water. Tuan saw his wife's face and shouted to her, "I will not join you, not today, my love." *Hold your breath with each giant wave, hold your kids, survive.* The fishing boat disappeared beneath the waves with the propeller still spinning.

Tuan kept as calm as he could manage, never loosening his grip on his children. He saw the shore, barely visible, boats now heading their way. He held on. Loan and Duc quiet, eyes huge, their shivering made him stronger. In less than an hour, a fishing boat appeared, strong arms pulled the three of them to safety. Shivering, he lay on the deck, thankful. They'd survived, America closer.

In Malaysia, they lingered for years, ending up on Bidong Island, a designated refugee camp in Malaysia. Less than one square mile across, the camp planned to accept no more than five-thousand refugees but ended up taking in forty-thousand who arrived on five-hundred boats. Relief and aid organizations helped ration food and water, and barely acceptable shelters made from old timbers, plastic sheeting, tin cans and palm fronds provided respite from the rain. The United States and other governments sent representatives to the island to interview refugees for resettlement. Tuan found odd jobs and saved everything he could for passage to America. At his interview, after one and a half years in Malaysia, he impressed the United States interviewer who granted approval for resettlement in the United States.

Tuan excitedly reported, "Kids, we're one step closer to America today!"

On one of Tuan's odd jobs, he met a man holding the hand of a small boy. Learning of Tuan's now real plans to emigrate to America, the man offered Tuan a proposal: take his son with them to America and when Tuan delivered the boy to his relatives in Los Angeles, they'd pay him $10,000 for his efforts. This was too good to be true, but Tuan landed on the idea with exuberance. The boy, named Ngoc, became Tuan's third and golden child in his journey to America.

Until the resettlement ship's departure date, uncertain but likely months away, Ngoc was treated as Tuan's child. Precious cargo, Ngoc received any food they had first. Ngoc received chicken with meat on the bones while Loan and Duc sucked on the bones that were left and the basis of their soup. Tuan knew that Ngoc's successful delivery as a healthy child was his ticket to success, and all measures and sacrifices had to be done for him. Ngoc was about five years old, Tuan's own children older. Loan and Duc understood the sacrifice and agreed. Ngoc would improve the family's chances of success in America.

A young U.S. representative hailed Tuan to the ship, told him to get ready in three hours. Tuan saw the 1500-ton freighter that would be their home for over a month. The ship, called Hai Hong, was an ugly gray behemoth, but beautiful because it would take them to America.

"This giant ship will take us to the land of plenty, the land where I will be paid $10,000 and where we begin a new, beautiful life," Tuan declared to his children.

Aboard, in the cramped quarters each had a cot and food. The big ship provided a much smoother voyage than the fishing boat that spilled them into the freezing water.

"A ship of this size will surely survive any mountainous waves," Tuan reasoned. He kept count of each day; on the thirty-second day, he heard cheers from those above. They'd sighted land.

America!

Leaving the boat, everything looked so big. The Port of Los Angeles resembled a museum of monsters: giant dinosaur cranes lined up, turned right, turned left, removing cargo off the gigantic ships. Rows and rows of containers stacked like a child's toy blocks, to Tuan, Loan, Duc, and Ngoc, a colorful welcome to the new land. Beyond the rows of containers, they could see an enormous lot with hundreds of gleaming new cars waiting for their new home in America, just like Tuan and his family. Tuan had never seen a new car in Vietnam, and never in Malaysia.

"This is a land of wealth, a place where people can buy new cars," a hopeful Tuan told his children.

Loaded onto busses, Tuan and his family, along with the rest of their shipmates, rode a long way to Camp Pendleton, California, where the International Rescue Mission helped process the refugees. After they welcomed the weary refugees to the United States, they worked to find them places to live.

Tuan felt so lucky, because his auntie lived in Los Angeles. At Camp Pendleton, his aunt's friend came to drive him and his family to Los Angeles. A one-bedroom apartment with Tuan's aunt, plus three other people, became a one-bedroom apartment with eight occupants. Tuan felt thankful to have a solid roof over his head. The windows closed. The door locked, and carpeting was underfoot. America impressed him already.

Tuan arranged transportation with a friend of his auntie to take Ngoc to his own people in downtown Los Angeles. He needed to collect the $10,000 that would make him a rich man and give him the start he needed in this new land. Loan and Duc stayed with their dad's aunt when Tuan took Ngoc to the LA address.

When they found the apartment on the third floor of an old brick four-story building off Wilshire Blvd., Tuan's heart beat hard in his chest when he knocked on the door with precious cargo Ngoc. The door opened, Ngoc's welcoming family scooped him up and hugged him so much he could hardly breathe. Ngoc gave his for-hire dad a quizzical glance. One of the women told them she'd bring tea, and after a respectable amount of time chatting about the journey, Tuan, with great courtesy, asked the elder in the room for the promised $10,000.

In raised voices, two of the relatives told Tuan in no uncertain terms, that they didn't have that kind of money, that Ngoc's family in Vietnam promised the $10,000, that they didn't promise anyone anything.

Shocked and angered, Tuan told them, his voice breaking in sobs, what they'd been through to get here.

"I protected Ngoc, treated him like my own son, gave him preference over my own children on this long journey. You owe this money to me! The family told me to collect the money from you! I delivered my end of the bargain."

"I can't help you! I'm not responsible for what Ngoc's father promised you. If you don't leave my home right now, I'll call the police," said the elder.

In frustration and reeling from the sense of betrayal, Tuan hit the elder in the face with his strong, travel-hardened fist. Ngoc's people piled on top of Tuan. Outnumbered, he and his driver managed to escape, run down three flights of stairs, and get to the car.

Driving back to his aunt's house, Tuan mumbled over and over to himself, "How could I have been such a fool?"

Back at the apartment, now with seven heads under one roof, Tuan knew he had to find work. The next week he walked the streets of downtown Los Angeles, block after block, thinking and looking. *What will I do?*

On the third day of walking the streets, Tuan saw what he thought was a Vietnamese man in a jewelry store. He went in, spoke Vietnamese to the gentleman, telling him his entire story. Tuan told this man he needed work to support his two children and help pay his part of the rent. The man, Minh, who happened to be the owner of the store, said that he'd like to hire another Vietnamese to work in his store because he'd recently lost an employee.

Tuan thanked Minh over and over, bowing and bowing, hiding the emotions threatening to make him cry. Tuan's job was to sweep the floors, clean the glass counters on both sides, and polish the lights. Sharp lights and clean glass made the jewelry attractive and brought in customers, he learned.

He worked at the jewelry store for several years. Minh came to depend on Tuan, giving him more and more responsibility. He trusted Tuan to pick up precious stones from the wholesalers, taught him how to value stones with a jeweler's loop, to look for imperfections, and later, how to set stones. Tuan learned the trade of a jeweler and took pride in all he learned, so pleased that Minh trusted him enough to charge him with his precious inventory.

Minh, at sixty-eight years of age and in good health, decided that he should retire and use the time to enjoy his years of hard work. He offered to sell his store to Tuan. Tuan saved a good portion of what he earned over the years, but certainly not enough to buy Minh's store from him. Minh offered to allow Tuan, who he now trusted like a son, to buy the store over time, with a down payment, then monthly payments until he paid the agreed-upon price in full. Ecstatic, Tuan jumped at the opportunity. He could now call himself a business owner in America, *the American Dream.*

The store Tuan bought thrived to the point that, in time, he opened another store in downtown LA, another in Glendora, and another in Torrance. He knew he had become an American success, and Tuan was determined to show it with gold and flashy cars. Having "made it," even without the promised $10,000 to get him started, humility eased into pride which flooded into excess.

His daughter Loan did well in high school. Upon graduation, California State University in Los Angeles accepted her for undergraduate studies, where she excelled with an over 4.0 grade point average. During her studies in science, she found herself interested in dentistry, a prestigious occupation, to her thinking, where she could concentrate on serving the Vietnamese community. Vietnamese communities, like many other minorities, did not have access to dental services; therefore, Loan felt this would be a good and profitable profession, plus one which would help her compatriots.

After dental school, Loan got her first job as a dentist at Golden Valley Health Center, where she concentrated in pediatric dentistry.

# CHAPTER 19

## LONG AND LOAN

Long's aggressive strategy to win Loan from his good-looking and wealthy competition, Duong, worked. Long's humility, discipline, intelligence, and sense of humor earned Loan's attention and eventually her heart. Important to Loan was Long's history—he came from an even humbler beginning than hers—he had made his success completely on his own, not as an entitled person with a family background of questionable ethics.

Long believed that he had to spend more of his savings on winning Loan. He took her to nice restaurants, spent time with her on weekends. Loan and Long's bond grew. They got to know each other well; in a few months, they knew they'd both fallen in love.

Loan wanted to introduce Long to her father, Tuan. Tuan had by then emerged from janitorial poverty to proud business owner, wore expensive chains, drove a flashy Mercedes sedan with gold wheels and custom leather interior. Tuan wanted only the best for his only daughter, Loan. She arranged to visit her father on a Saturday, where Long would submit to an interview with Tuan. In Vietnamese culture, a daughter's father had to approve of potential husbands for her.

After picking up Loan, Long arrived at Tuan's huge Mediterranean home in eastern Los Angeles, Loan introduced him to her father. They shook hands, bowed slightly. Tuan grunted his answer, when Long said, "I am so pleased to meet you."

After tea and polite conversation, Tuan summoned Long to his den with dark wood bookshelves lining three walls under a ten-foot ceiling and a gleaming mahogany desk in the middle of the room. Tuan sat behind the desk, dwarfed in his massive leather chair, reading glasses over his nose. He gave Long several suspicious once-overs. Long wore a clean, pressed suit.

Long spoke first: "I am interested in Loan and want to move the relationship to the next level."

Tuan stared over his reading glass lenses at the shy young man but said nothing. Instead, Tuan, palm outward, shook his head. Those gestures, Long knew, meant meeting over, a bust.

Long knew that he did not close the deal. His over-modest demeanor, his ten-year-old shabby Datsun B 210 parked out front, his failure to bring his financial plan resulted in failure, outright. He had a lot of work to do.

A month later, Loan told Long her father extended a second invitation to the house. This time, Long brought a copy of his savings and checking accounts, and once again faced Tuan in his den.

"I drive a modest car and have a modest manner of dress, but I have money, Long said. "To show you, I've brought you my savings and checking account statements. Together they equal over $20,000." Long felt proud of his savings, because he'd started from zero. To his surprise, Tuan's hand once again shot up, with the now familiar wave-off. Long left the room disappointed and defeated. *What went wrong?*

Through Loan's persuasion, Tuan extended yet a third invitation for Long to plead his case after several months. This time, he armed himself not only with his checking account statements and his savings account, he brought along his stock portfolio, which now boasted a substantial $100,000, plus the $20,000 of Long's personal accounts. Long's net worth had reached $120,000.

In the den, same chair in front of Tuan's desk, where Tuan was comfortably seated, Long laid out each of the documents plus a clear spreadsheet before him on the polished desk

"Sir, I arrived in the U.S. an orphan. I had nothing. But I had the opportunity of landing in America, pockets empty. I made my own way. These documents show you what I 've amassed and though I have a modest car, I owe no debt, own the car outright."

Tuan's expression went from the skeptic to friend. He grunted to himself, nodded, stood up, made his way around the massive desk, motioned Long to stand up, and gave Long a tight bear hug.

Long, surprised, sheepishly hugged back, suppressing the desire to break down in sobs, knowing his hard work had paid off.

"Welcome to the family, Long!" Tuan said.

Long grinned until his face ached, subdued his impulse to leap around the room. He'd won Loan—he'd won the woman he loved.

# CHAPTER 20

# CAREER: EARN MONEY TO INVEST

Tuan threw his daughter a huge, flashy wedding with many guests. Afterwards, the happy couple settled down in Merced, California.

Long worked for a major health technology company and became their chief operating officer for worldwide operations. Loan bought, built up, then sold her lucrative dental practice before they moved to Southern California to live near her family: her father and brother. There they'd raise the family they dreamt of.

Loan earned millions through the sale of her dental practice up north, and Long invested every penny of his salary according to his financial plan.

Today, this couple is worth in excess of fifty million dollars. And Long's goal now? Amass $100 million through careful investing.

With their two children now at universities earning honors, one in engineering and one in pre-medicine, Long and Loan like to travel. Hong Kong is one of their favorites—the glistening lights, superior food, and world-class hotels. They love to stroll the boulevards late at night, dressed up just a little. Every now and then, Long will notice a discarded can of soda on the street, and instinctively, pick up this treasure, crush it in his hand, and put it in his pocket. Returned for cash, more money to invest.

Long and Loan took one their favorite strolls down Park Lane Shopper's Boulevard on a recent trip to Hong Kong, when Long noticed a couple walking the opposite direction. He looked at them because they seemed so happy, laughing, holding hands. Long the Observer looked at them and his heart raced. *Could it be?* thought Long. He looked closer and was now sure. Long and Loan walked up to them and he asked, "Are you Ba Phuong?"

"Yes."

"I'm Long! White Peanut!"

"Oh my god! It's you! I worried so much and hoped and that you and Duc would be all right after the end of the war."

They hugged for a long time, just like Long remembered.

"This is Loan, my wife!"

"This is Danh, my husband. We live here now. How is Duc?"

Long's face went blank. He didn't know how to tell her. "I'm sorry…he was killed in a car accident over 25 years ago."

Ba Phuong started to cry. "Oh my god, that is terrible."

"They say his organs saved three people," Long said softly, still proud of his big brother.

"I am so sad. So sad! I loved that boy, my 'Black Peanut,' just as I loved you as my own. When I lost you boys, my world ended. No one knew anything, where you went, whether you were ok. I tried for years to get information, but there was none. I ran to where the American trucks were taking the children, but they wouldn't let me in. I hoped that you and Duc were there and were ok."

Long looked at Ba with understanding. Every night he said goodnight to Duc before going to sleep—out loud if alone, to himself if not.

She was as beautiful as Long remembered. Seeing Ba Phuong filled an emptiness Long didn't realize he had.

He had found his mother.

# AUTHOR'S NOTE

My own story with Long began in 2007. I was having a difficult time finding a new finance director for my company. I'd interviewed half-a-dozen candidates— none proved to be "the one." The seventh candidate, a humble, professionally dressed, small-in-stature Asian gentleman was shown into my office by the Human Resources Director. I asked the usual questions: his background, how he would solve some of the problems my company was facing, and what he thought about the industry in general.

Within twenty minutes of talking with Long, I knew I had found that competent, knowledgeable person I wanted. He made me feel comfortable that he was there to do the job, and do it extremely well. During the interview, I felt the strength of his discernment and character; he was not just looking for a job but also to work with someone who had the same heart. I could *feel* his evaluation of me, and I could feel that connection when we concluded the interview.

I walked out of my office after the interview and said to one of my executives, "I have found the one!" I don't know why, but when I said that, I fought back tears of joy. In love or business, when you've finally found the right fit, you *just know*, and with Long I did.

I checked references. One after the other affirmed my instincts: "I would hire him back in a minute"; "The only reason we are not still working together is he had to relocate for his family"; and more. I never experienced references like that—their accolades for Long were honest, unrehearsed, and heartfelt. I felt extremely good about my decision to make an offer.

Long proved to be a remarkable employee. Collaborative, effective, direct, and a great presenter of the facts, no matter how difficult. The one small criticism I came across in my reference checks was that he was perceived as quiet in meetings, rarely speaking up. He was blending in, but always there, always engaged, always absorbing. Like "Radar" on the TV hit *Mash*, he knew what I wanted before I did. "How about a report on....?" Boom. There. Done.

He had a quiet sense of humor that he doled out sparingly over the years I worked with him. He called the report he simplified for management the "Fisher-Price" model with colors and graphs so that they grab your attention and are easily understood. While he dubbed it the "Fisher-Price" model, it was very sophisticated with considerable thought and analysis behind it.

He proved to be "as described" by his former associates, and for the ten years we worked together, he helped me run the company as my right hand. Then, at the right time, he helped me sell it through a long and sophisticated process, for a fair price.

Today he's worth almost $50 million, accumulated quietly.

He did it by investing consistently and wisely. He did not become wealthy via his profession, salary, stock grants, or bonuses. He accomplished it by living extremely frugally, shopping in second-hand clothing stores or the day-old section of the grocery store, and driving a 10-year-old Toyota mini-van. Any movies he would watch with his children growing up were free rentals from the library. Books the children read were loaned, not purchased. He continues to live this way today, except for his passion for traveling with his wife and children. They love Mexico (all-inclusive resorts, of course) and Asia – Vietnam, Thailand, Hong Kong – and go as often as possible.

Family is the single most important thing to Long, nurturing and cherishing what he never had growing up.

In our time together, Long imparted his life story along with some very judicious life and investment advice. The following is an encapsulated version of Long's investment thinking.

### "Companies That Will Outlive Me" – Long's Four Strategic Investing Principles

- **Recurring revenue** is revenue that is not transactional, like selling a shirt, but earns continually, such as a service contract for Dell on top of the one-time sale of a PC. When Dell sells servers, they also sell a service contract, which means recurring revenue for the company. Cyber security earns recurring revenue because of upgrades in response to new cyber threats. They earn monthly fees to do this. Visa and Mastercard are also built on recurring revenue. Every transaction, on any Visa or Mastercard, regardless of which bank's name is on the card, earns recurring revenue for Visa or Mastercard. They profit from providing infrastructure to banks and financial institutions throughout the world that use Visa and Mastercard's processing platform. As the world economy grows, so do Visa and mastercard.

- **No debt** is a company culture that avoids debt. If there is debt, it is for good reason and not to augment cash flow. Visa, for example, recently bought Visa Europe, incurring debt for that transaction. This purchase is good debt because the company generates cash flow from Visa Europe and pays off the original debt from that. Apple used debt to buy stock back, which is also an exception to the rule. This is known as a tax mitigation strategy. They pay 2.5% for debt to buy their own stock which is growing at 15% per year. The recent retail bankruptcies of Toys R Us, JC Penny, and Sears happened in part because of their handling of debt and leverage. Venture firms bought some of these companies, issued debt against them, and the debt service killed their profitability—and therefore the businesses. In simple terms, these companies had loans to pay, and when their business went down due to online competition, they still had to pay the loans with less revenue coming in.

- **High margin** refers to companies with high margins relative to the industry they are in. With high margin, debt avoidance, and recurring revenue, the company can ride out any recession. The company will end up stronger than competitors without these characteristics. Weak competitors will go out of business, as they have to pay their debt regardless of a market downturn.

- **Trustworthy brand and management** are key to success. Strong companies have strong, ethical leaders. Do research on their writings, stories written about their management style, look at YouTube to hear them speak. For example, watch Jamie Dimon, CEO of JP Morgan Chase, speaking at Stanford University. Observe at him at the Davos, Switzerland conference. Look at the CEO's behavior, how they answer questions, and use your intuition to assess them.

  Research the CEO's prior positions and their successes, who they are and what they did before. Look to see if other key executives remain at the company after the CEO is appointed—keeping the brainpower and institutional knowledge has value. If executives leave, it is a bad sign—the brain trust is leaving. Look at the careers section of the company's website and see if they are hiring, a sign of planned growth. Look at the reputation of the company. Apple is well known for its ethical behavior, for example. Other companies might have significant litigation in progress, another marker to consider. Do a Google search on the company to see what stories are being written, positive or negative, to get a better picture of the company as an investment target.

## Long's Investment Strategies – "Words of Wisdom"

- "When investing, control your emotions from the day you start to the day you finish."

- "Listening to Jim Cramer and other pundits can get you in trouble if you're chasing headlines. If you're in solid companies, you won't be rewarded right away, but you win in the long run."

- "Invest what you earn from solid companies. You can't listen to the noise."

- "The hardest thing is mastering *discipline*. Feeling left out because you missed something shows a weakness that hinders your investment success."

- "Knowing the company you want to invest in is critically important."

  For example, Dell proved to be one of Long's wins. He watched the company transition from a personal computer company to a server company. Dell has a negative revenue cycle, meaning that they get paid before they produce the product. Dell built their website so consumers can customize their PC to their liking. The customer pays Dell with a credit card, *then and only then do they build* the PC and deliver it a month later. Therefore, there is no inventory to maintain and no negative cash flow. Dell became the first computer business to do this.

Apple, at the time, built their computers for consumers, carried a large inventory, and customers had to go into one of their stores to buy the product. Dell created "just in time production." Dell was more of a logistics company than a PC company. Dell cashed out their investors when they decided to become a private company versus being a publicly traded company. When they paid Long for the stock he owned, he took that money and bought seven houses in Riverside, California, for cash, as investments.

• What makes Long look at a company in the first place? First, luck. "Luck only comes if you're looking for it." Long uses libraries. He finds more substance if he reads print as opposed to the internet. Long picks up magazines, reads articles, gets ideas. For example, he's currently researching block chain technology. If he finds information in a magazine, he knows that editors have reviewed and confirmed credibility, whereas on the internet, anyone can post. He finds Barron's complicated and boring. Long likes simple. What does he study? Data, data, data—graphs, bar charts, history, and of course, the leadership.

- I asked Long, "If you taught your knowledge to your son or daughter, how would you do it?"

  "Your life upbringing gives you different motivations," he replied. "They could learn it technically using my four principles and narrow four thousand companies down to twenty, but the interpretation, the intuition, can't be taught. Their upbringing and lifestyle affect the analysis."

  His intuition is not teachable. He emphasizes, "Controlling your emotions is always critical." For example, to have the ability to ride out the market during recessions, you have to live frugally, have cash to ride it out. "If possible, don't have a mortgage, debt. Do have liquidity so you can ride things out. You have to be set up decades in advance to prepare yourself for this way of living and investing. Stay away from trends, such as the .com boom in the late 90's. Don't zig when everyone else is. Prepare to zag. For example, number one and hardest, maintaining discipline."

When stocks crash based on the news, such as China boycotting Apple, people sold off Apple. Not Long. In the 2008 recession, Long rode it out because he set himself up for it. During the recession, he realized that the banks that survived, such as JP Morgan Chase, and Wells Fargo, would be good investments.

"Recessions come and go, that's natural. Even 1930, if you step back and look at the charts, it shows recessions correct themselves in the long term." Framed on Long's office wall are three Wall Street Journal front page graphs, each for a different decade, each showing that over a ten-year or more period of time, the trend is always upward. You must be prepared for the bumps downward because they are temporary.

• Another example of Long's well-thought-out analysis: Cerner, a healthcare information technology company, partnered with Amazon Web Services. With Amazon's obvious reach, this partnership bodes well for both companies, but Wall Street has not yet recognized this partnership. Google is hiring some exceptional healthcare people; Cerner has significant healthcare data, so it will add to the value of Cerner when Google begins seeking healthcare data for its efforts. Cerner bought back their own stock at $63 per share in big chunks, even when Cerner sold at $59 in the open market. Cerner buying back a billion of its own stock is good indicator, especially if they are paying a premium of $4 per share. Cerner recently was sold to Oracle for $95 per share.

- Another of Long's rules, but you must have liquidity to do this: buy during a "sale," when you see a big market correction downward. For example, when the market went down significantly one day, while Long was taking a walk on the pier in Huntington Beach, California, he looked at his phone and saw that JP Morgan Chase was also down for the day (one of his holdings). He also saw that one of Warren Buffet's two top lieutenants, Todd Combs, bought a huge junk of JP Morgan Chase for himself. On the spot,

Long bought $76,000 worth of JP Morgan Chase on his phone while on the pier. With this bargain price in his mind, loading up on stocks that will "outlast him" makes sense. Todd was "trained by the master, Warren Buffet."

Why did Long happen to be taking a walk at the beach? He had a coupon for a free oil change nearby and was killing time at the beach while mechanics worked on his car. "Watch every penny. A penny not spent is a penny you can invest."

- Another example of Long's research was finding that JP Morgan Chase has a subsidiary called Chasepaymentech, which provides the transaction systems behind Visa and Mastercard. They process $1 trillion transactions annually. For example, when a customer checks out and pushes "Buy Now" at Amazon, the payment processor behind it—that links Visa, Mastercard, or American Express to Amazon—happens to be Chasepaymentech. As online purchasing continues to grow, so will Chasepaymentech, now called Chase Merchant Services. Long believes this should be worth much more but stays hidden inside of JP Morgan Chase.

- Long has also analyzed the company Square, run by Twitter founder Jack Dorsey, who runs both companies. Visa owns 20% of Square. It has good management, and a good company concept: technology for small companies, and credible large investors.

- "If you manage stocks yourself, you don't have act like a fund manager who has clients who all want to sell when the market's down. When clients want to sell, fund managers need to sell to get cash to pay clients, further driving down the fund's price. Funds have stops put in, guaranteeing that losses won't be excessive. To the extent that most funds have that kind of stop, it builds and drives the market down further." Managing stocks yourself, you can ride out market downturns and even buy more at a reduced price.

NOTES: Any reference to particular stocks is only to provide examples and is not a recommendation to buy or to sell.

Characters' names in this book may have been changed to protect their privacy.

# ABOUT THE AUTHOR

Bruce Carlin is an accomplished executive in the healthcare and retail industries. He started his own company in 1998, focused on delivering healthcare as a consumer service rather than the cold and disjointed product it has been historically. Long worked alongside him, an unassuming but diligent professional who applied wise financial analysis to Carlin's company. After ten years together, Carlin began piecing together snippets of his colleague's fascinating life story as an orphan immigrant who overcame extraordinary obstacles. Then, with Long's approval, Carlin decided to write this American success story and share it with others. The book's lesson to all is if you want something, you must remain ***Undeterred.***

Made in the USA
Columbia, SC
22 October 2022

69828481R00093